classic mosaic

classic mosaic

DESIGNS & PROJECTS
INSPIRED BY 6,000
YEARS OF MOSAIC ART

elaine m. goodwin

"MOSAIC: A MYRIAD
OF FRAGMENTS,
EACH FRAGMENT AN
INSPIRATION."

EMG

McArthur & Company

Toronto

acknowledgments

During my research, production, and writing, I have been helped by many – I thank them all: the officials and assorted guides in museums and galleries, at public sites and churches and in distant cities and far-flung desert areas; material manufacturers; mosaic scholars; mosaicists and friends. In connection with the projects, I thank Maurice Stapley, Vic Mousel, Margot Lublinski, Tony Wheaton, and Dave Head. For his geometric drawings, my thanks to Bob Field and for photographs, advice, and support, my thanks to John Melville. A special thank-you to Jonathan Russell Read for his creative camera work in connection with the projects. For special mention, my grateful thanks to Lindy Ayubi, who with constant and tireless enthusiasm realized the text for me from unintelligible scribbles to the mysterious sophistication of a computer disk. As ever, warm thanks to my wondrous Group 5.

picture credits

The author and publisher would like to acknowledge and thank the following for permission to reproduce their images:

AKG London page 22; AKG London/Stefan Drechsel page 20 (top); AKG London/Erich Lessing pages 70, 92; AKG London/Giles Mermet page 87; G. Blore page 48; British Museum pages 78, 120; e.t. archive pages 9, 16 (top), 17; Robert Field page 11; Elaine M. Goodwin 2, 12 (top), 14, 15, 16 (bottom), 19, 20 (bottom), 21, 25, 26, 28, 29 (top), 30, 31, 34 (left), 36 (top right), 54 (bottom left), 83, (top left), 96 (left), 104 (left), 112 (left), 116 (left), 124 (left), 144; Elaine M. Goodwin/Robert Field page 24; Elaine M. Goodwin/John Melville page 29 (bottom); H. Kudo page 31 (bottom); Life File/Xavier Catalan page 24–5 (bottom); Life File/Sue Davies page 133; Mondadori Archives page 12 (bottom), 23; L. Orsoni page 31 (top); Michele Piccirillo page 18, 100; Raw Vision/Maggie Jones Maizels page 27; The Bridgeman Art Library page 13; The Bridgeman Art Library/Ali Meyer page 128.

Canadian Cataloguing in Publication Data
Goodwin, E. M. (Elaine M.)
    Classic mosaic: designs and projects inspired by 6,000
    years of mosaic art.
Includes bibliographical references.

ISBN 1-55278-123-2

1. Mosaics – Technique. 2. Mosaics – History. I. Title.
NA3750.G66 2000   738.5   C99-932808-5

A QUINTET BOOK
This book was designed and produced by
Quintet Publishing Limited
6 Blundell Street, London N7 9BH

Creative Director: Richard Dewing
Art Director: Silke Braun
Designer: James Lawrence
Project Editors: Carine Tracanelli
                Doreen Palamartschuk
Editor: Andrew Armitage
Photographers: John Melville, Jonathan Russell Read
Typeset in Great Britain by
Central Southern Typesetters, Eastbourne
Manufactured in Hong Kong by
Regent Publishing Services Ltd
Printed in Singapore by Star Standard Industries (Pte) Ltd.

safety notice

Mosaic making can be dangerous, and readers should follow safety procedures, and wear protective clothing and goggles, at all times during the preparation of tesserae and the making and fitting of mosaics. Neither the author, copyright holders nor publishers of this book can accept legal liability for any damage or injury sustained as a result of making mosaics.

contents

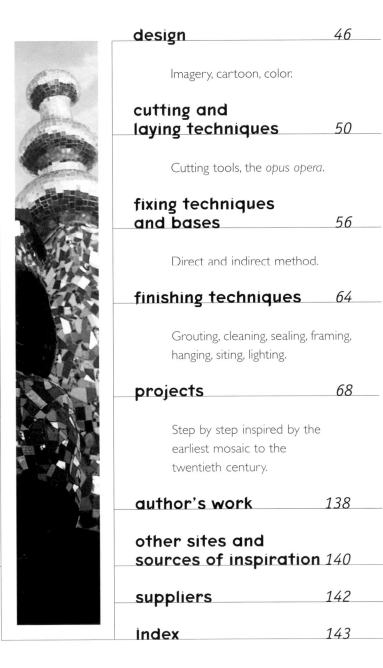

introduction

about the book
The inspiration for compiling this book comes directly from observing mosaics from their earliest beginnings up to the present day.

The 16 projects explore the values that aroused delight, curiosity, and wonder. Each project develops an understanding into the material used, the position it holds, whether on ceiling, floor, wall, or object, and the reasoning behind the design – practical, spiritual, functional or decorative.

You will be encouraged to make original mosaics, not slavishly from identical templates or as a piece-by-piece facsimile, but in the spirit of their creation. In absorbing the techniques and methods used today, you should be confident to create original and exciting designs for all situations, including domestic interiors, gardens, exteriors, and public locations. In this way you will become a direct descendant of the mosaic makers of history, using mosaic to adorn, to decorate, and to depict the imagery and spirit of the day.

about the author
Elaine M. Goodwin has traveled all over the world through her love of mosaic. She was tutor for several years in mosaic art and design in Exeter and London in England, and has continued as visiting tutor to several organizations in India, Australia, England, Italy, and Greece. Her work includes the book *Decorative Mosaics,* a video, *Making a Mosaic,* feature articles in *World of Interiors, Country Living, BBC Homes and Antiques,* and other magazines, and television programs. In 1994 she was elected as member of the Associazione Internazionale Mosaicisti Contemporanei (AIMC). Her work is rich in symbolism and the treasures found in mosaics handed down through the centuries.

what is a mosaic?
A mosaic is a work made up of cut fragments with no particular identity. These cut pieces – which may be made of glass, shell, stone, or china – are assembled together with a binding agent but with gaps left between them. When a mosaic is completed it gains an identity either through a recognizable image or an abstract design.

It is an additive medium – one piece follows another – and has been used at least since the fourth millennium BC in this way to decorate and express the needs and feelings of people, both publicly and domestically. It is a wonderful medium and can utilize the simplest and the most luxurious of materials: stones, pebbles, glass, and gold. It has always held a fascination for people, and its versatile nature can be adapted to a wide range of needs. Practical, beautiful, forceful, enduring, magical, awesome – it can be all these things, but above all it holds the power to inspire admiration and imitation.

a short history of mosaic

ancient babylon Over five thousand years ago in present-day Iraq at Uruq/Warka, that most ancient of Sumerian cities, hundreds and thousands of clay cones shaped like bullets were pressed into a wet mud plaster to strengthen and decorate the walls of the city's great temples and sanctuaries to create a mosaic surface. From these ancient beginnings mosaic has continued to combine the practical with the beautiful: a combination that has inspired emperors, kings, artists, artisans, and householders to express their feelings and ideas.

Early use of materials such as lapis lazuli, shell, terracotta, onyx, and other hard stones has decorated furniture, columns, and portable pieces very much in the same way that might be found in a mosaic of today.

▼ **Standard of Ur, Sumeria, third millennium** BC, **British Museum, London, England.**
This consists of two flanked panels, each divided into three registers, one side having an imagery of war, the other side of peace. It is made of semiprecious stones and shell. It is not a mosaic in any real sense, but is an example of a related inlay technique called Opus Sectile. *The borders have panels of tiny squared pieces of shell, continuing an early decorative application.*

9

ancient greece

Pebbles have been used since Neolithic times to provide a serviceable, hard-wearing surface for walking on, both as external paving and interior flooring. The need to combine function with design can be seen in the way that many of these extant surfaces are patterned, even if very simply, with geometric designs, simple color combinations, and variation in the size of the pebbles. During the fifth century BC, mosaics made of light pebbles on dark grounds of red, green, blue, and black pebbles, loosely laid and relying heavily on carpet imagery, occur at Olynthos in the Chalcidice, Greece. The imagery is mythological and is executed in a lively manner. Other pebble mosaics can be seen at Paphos on the island of Cyprus, and at Eretria on the island of Evia (Euboea) in Greece, where the elegant designs are from the fourth century BC. Two of the mosaics represent mythological scenes with borders of floral patterning and vegetal ornament.

The most sophisticated designs are to be found at Pella, in Macedonia in Greece, and can be dated to the late fourth century BC. Apart from the exquisite floral borders, they are inspired by paintings of the period and rely on creating an illusion of three-dimensional space on the flat pebble surface. The artists, among them the first known and named mosaicist Gnosis, chose smaller and smaller pebbles to "sculpt" the forms and give them the appearance of painted reality. Lead strips are occasionally inserted to help contour the forms of hunters and animals. The imagery includes an Amazonomachy, a lion and stag hunt, and a possible representation of Alexander the Great and his friend Krateros.

The choosing of smaller pebbles to create the illusion of reality within the mosaic led to a gradual transition into using cut stone or marble. At first the pebbles were chipped and shaped for greater definition, and later it became more economical to prepare rectangular rods of stone from which individual small cubes, called *tesserae* (plural of *tessera*), could be cut and used as required. This change from natural pebble to deliberately cut stone gave greater control over the material, and a mosaic with a tessellated surface of intended color and unit size was born.

◄ **Dionysus on a Panther, Pella, Macedonia, Greece, fourth century BC.**
One of the most delicately rendered pebble mosaics is of a youthful Dionysus, god of fertility, riding on one of his attributes, a panther. The tones are soft and gently shaded to hint at a three-dimensional form. The lines are sinuous and seem to deny the hard surface of the pebble.

greco-roman Early examples of specifically cut tesserae are found wherever the Greek culture had spread: on Delos in the Greek islands; in Sicily in Italy; at Alexandria in Egypt; and at Pergamum in present-day Turkey. The designs were originally inspired by carpets and came to be represented by a central panel with surrounding borders.

The central part of the mosaic was made away from the site in a workshop or *officina*, and was of much smaller tesserae. Frequently figurative, it was made up on a slab of marble or terracotta, and, when completed, inserted into a space left for it in the center of a design. This portable panel was called the *emblema*. The *emblemata* (plural) were of many colors and were finely executed, with some sections of tesserae consisting of small contour-like lines — *Opus Vermiculatum* — like little worms (*vermi* in Latin), which followed a curve or a shading line. They were often very detailed, and the images were modulated with tone and direction, (*andamento*), to look like paintings in stone, thus continuing the Hellenistic practice of imitating painting.

The surrounding borders were created directly on site, and were often made up of larger cubes of stone and marble and in a variety of geometric or border patterns from a Greek tradition of motifs, including wave crests, meanders, cubes, and checkers.

The Romans in Imperial Rome regarded mosaics of this type as luxury items. Many fine examples from wealthy villas come from discoveries made at Pompeii and Herculaneum in Southern Italy. Pompeii was buried under volcanic ash from the eruption of Mount Vesuvius in AD 79. The mosaic examples rescued are therefore known to have been made before this date.

The refined emblemata made and executed by Greek mosaicists were used abundantly in Pompeii. These luxurious and colorful items embellished the villas of the wealthy patrician classes. The Romans adapted the imagery to their taste, with battles ranking foremost — whether between great leaders, as in the Battle of Issus in which Alexander the Great confronts Darius III of Persia, or between smaller beings, such as a cat and a quail, or a lobster and an octopus.

▶ **Drawings by Bob Field, 1998, showing a Greco-Roman mosaic border pattern.**
The shield-like pelta *design can be developed in numerous ways, creating different effects or shapes.*

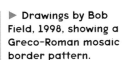

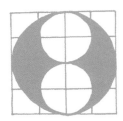

the romans

The fashion for mosaic grew in Italy from the early second century, and a new style of mosaic emerged to meet the Roman taste and fashion. This was a much simpler black-and-white style. Mosaic was not only to be owned by the wealthy who could afford the elaborate polychromatic emblemata, but it was also needed to decorate new communal places like public baths – or *thermae* – as well as shops and houses. Monochromatic mosaics were considerably cheaper and quicker to make. Two-color mosaics required much simpler techniques – designs using black tesserae were created on white grounds using much larger cubed pieces, and backgrounds were filled in with rows of horizontal and vertical tesserae, *Opus Tessellatum*.

Popular images of dolphins, marine life, and sea mythology occur at the Roman port of Ostia, which was a great center of black-and-white mosaic work, and at the Baths of Caracalla, Rome. Images that reflect Roman life are also to be found, such as athletic games, hunting, and circus spectacles. By reflecting the way people lived, images in this medium were detached from any connections with painting and became more immediate, lively, striking, and original.

Not all mosaics in the Roman period were floor mosaics. Walls were also known to have had mosaic surfaces. The rear courtyards of the villas of Pompeii and Herculaneum often served as summer dining rooms where fountains and *nymphaea* – shrines to the gods – were decorated with water motifs made of shells, glass, and stone. Mosaics should not be seen in isolation – they were one part of a complete decorative scheme that included frescoes, wall paintings, and molded cornices. They were also seen as symbols of status, both in wealth and in taste.

▲ **Nilotic mosaic, Pompeii, Italy, first century** AD.
One of the most eloquent emblema is of the exotica of the Nile. The Romans had conquered Egypt in 30 BC and were entranced by the flora and fauna of the great river. The imagery is again of conflict – cobra and mongoose, hippo and crocodile – but overall the imagery abounds in a well-observed Nilotic scene.

◄ **Cupid on a marine animal (detail), Thermae of Caracalla, Rome, Italy, third century** AD.
The figure is silhouetted against a white background. The anatomical details are defined with strong white lines. The tesserae are large, often ¾ in/1.5 cm square, and the effect is lively and vigorous.

▲ **Rear Courtyard, Herculaneum, Italy,
first century BC.**
*The wall mosaic above is of Neptune, god of the ocean,
surrounded by a mosaic of shell design and a frame of real
shells. The rear wall mosaic is a nymphaeum and has an
elegant decorative scheme of climbing vines and hunting.
It is also framed in shells, probably from the shores of
Herculaneum, an ancient Roman seaside resort.*

the spread of rome
As the Roman Empire expanded so too did the use of mosaic decoration. All around the Mediterranean and North Africa, in Europe and in Britain, there evolved flourishing mosaic centers. Each Roman province established workshops – or *officinae* – which drew inspiration from popular taste and local artistic tradition, combined with a cross-sharing of pattern books and traveling master mosaicists. Though essentially Roman in concept and in character, each province developed a highly individual *oeuvre* of mosaic work characterized by differences in virtuosity, color, and decorative and stylistic features.

roman britain
In Roman Britain, the Empire's farthest province, mosaics are known to have existed since AD 60. The earliest fragments are from a legionary bathhouse in Isca Dumnoniorum (Exeter) and show lively polychromatic figurative features. There is an underlying tendency in Roman Britain to contain mosaic imagery within a geometric framework. This is sometimes realized as richly textural, or as mathematical with optical detail, or even with black-and-white simplicity.

◄ **Orpheus mosaic, Withington, Gloucestershire, England, fourth century AD** – drawing from **Samuel Lysons, 1817**.
A naïve and lively rendering of the Orphic theme with big animals, including a wild boar, bear, and panther running around the centrally placed mythical god of music and poetry. The birds, instead of encircling the figure as in other Orpheus mosaics, appear in the border.

Figurative imagery is conservative and various, including the four seasons and classical and mythological representations. In the British Museum in London there is a mosaic, originally from Durnovaria (Dorchester), of the earliest known portrait of Christ on a floor mosaic. Another collection, of which at least 14 are known, is the group of Orpheus mosaics, often using a uniquely conceived concentric circular design of beautifully studied and represented animals and birds, arranged around a centrally placed Orpheus figure.

tunisia and north africa
In the Roman province of Northern Africa – present-day Tunisia, Algeria, Libya, and Morocco – many schools, or *officinae*, of mosaic flourished. They were concentrated particularly in Carthage (in Tunisia), which was an important gateway and center to outside influence from Rome and later from Byzantium. During the six centuries of Roman domination, North Africa developed a colorful and thoroughly Romanized way of life, as expressed in the numerous mosaic pavements that have been excavated and well preserved. One decorative scheme that had its roots in Hellenistic emblemata is that of hospitality or *xenia*. Gastronomic representations and complete menus of delicious fruits and culinary delights embellished the floors of well-to-do citizens. Baskets of cherries, pears, and figs, trussed-up birds and fowl (including a flamingo), flagons and amphorae of wine – all testify to the many benefits enjoyed by the wealthy under Roman rule. **Roman power was omnipresent.** Property and lands were imperially owned or privately managed. Wealth was in large part accrued by agricultural practice.

The stability and wealth arising from long Roman occupation is shown in a way of life that survives in the imagery of many mosaic themes, for example athletic games and spectacles (since more than half the year was taken up with public holidays). Mosaics of myths, muses, the seasons, and the cult of Dionysus proliferate, and many mosaics rely on the decorative qualities of pattern. Designs were suffused in Roman ideology through symbol and image. North Africa has probably the richest legacy of mosaics depicting a totally Roman provincial lifestyle with all its magnificence, diversity, and desires.

▲ **The Estate of Lord Julius, Bardo Museum, Tunisia, fourth to fifth century** AD.

The mosaic records life on an imperial estate. The owner's imposing castle home is centrally placed and surrounded by pictures of his tenants and workers hunting, paying rent, and gathering fruits from the richly laden trees and estate lands. Amusingly, the landlord's wife, lower left, is shown in a posture reminiscent of many of the Venus depictions. She is portrayed with the attributes of Venus, is surrounded by roses, and holds a mirror while being offered her jewelry. In this case, however, she is luxuriantly clothed – unlike Venus, who is generally depicted as luxuriously nude.

italy

It is thought that North African artists, with their delight in portraying the good life, were brought over to work on the vast pavements of a luxurious villa in Casale in Sicily (Piazza Armerina). They decorated about 4,000 square yards (over 3,500 square meters) of floor, documenting big-game hunting, and reproducing scenes from mythology, such as the labors of Hercules. These are shown intermingled with mosaics in lighter vein depicting cupids or *putti* at play. The whole testifies to a highly developed and sophisticated lifestyle initiated by a wealthy villa owner of the third or fourth century, thought to be Emperor Maximianus Herculius.

The change from a pagan world to a Christian one in terms of imagery was that of a natural evolution – an adoption of images with a converted significance. This is clearly seen in Rome in the circular mausoleum of Santa Costanza. It is immediately apparent that the mosaics are on a vaulted ceiling, a more suitable place for religious imagery than underfoot.

▲ **Santa Costanza, Rome, Italy. Detail from the ceiling, fourth century** AD.
The background is of white marble, while variously colored glass tesserae have been used to create the brightly glowing and amusing images of the foliage and birds.

The many motifs on a white background recall the Unswept Floor mosaics of the Greek tradition. Colorful birds and vases are interspersed with scenes of vine harvesting and wine pressing undertaken by lively *putti*. All is conceived in a delightful, richly colored pagan – or conversely Christian – mosaic representing the Vineyard of the Lord of Christianity.

◄ **Playful Cupid among the marine creatures, Piazza Armerina, Sicily, third to fourth century** AD.
The lively and busy sea full of fish and water creatures recalls the menu-like fish imagery of the Greek emblemata. The treatment of the tesserae depicting water with zigzag forms and short lines of lozenge-shaped tesserae is similar to the paving of North Africa and also to the Paleochristian pavements of Aquileia in northeast Italy, where the imagery of fish is suggestive of Christians in a pagan world.

early byzantine

Constantinople or Byzantium (present day Istanbul), was founded in 330 AD under the dominion of the Christian emperor Constantine the Great. Mosaic work was much encouraged – mosaicists being exempt from taxation – and a school of mosaic was formed around the Bosphorus. The monumental church of Hagia Sophia preserves a few fragments of mosaic from this time.

The two changes, of lifting mosaics from the floor to the ceiling and utilizing glass material to create glowing areas of color and luminescence, were to be exploited to the full in the mosaics of the aspiring religion of Christianity over the following centuries.

In AD 402 the seat of the Western Roman Empire was moved to Ravenna in northeastern Italy. Previously a small provincial town, Ravenna became transformed with important buildings which, under the aegis of Justinian, the Byzantine emperor, took on an oriental aspect. The austere external beauty of the buildings – churches, mausoleums, and baptisteries – belies their sumptuous interiors, interiors that used mosaic art in a new guise, adapted to proclaim a new faith, Christianity.

Walls, apses, and vaulting were encrusted with mosaics, not of stone and marble but of glass – a particular glass made especially for mosaic work called *smalti*. Its properties were many: it was durable, it had a brilliance when light caught its cut surface, and it was colorful. Its color range was radiant with all possible nuances of greens, blues, yellows, reds, violets, whites, and gold.

The properties of glass, with areas of shifting light and color change, allowed an interior to become a space where the humble suppliant was transported into a spiritual realm, and where the world of naturalism and reality was left behind. So the imagery began to change from intensely observed nature, as beloved of the Greeks and the Romans, into a more abstract form of expression. It is in the church of San Vitale that Byzantine mosaic begins to find its fullest expression. Figures are no longer conceived naturalistically, but are conceived as symbols in an ordered hierarchical scheme.

The mosaics of Jordan are represented by Classical, Byzantine, and the Umayyad eras, spanning a period from the third to the seventh century AD. They developed stylistically and individually in response to an enduring classical taste. The mosaics adopted and adapted a rich repertoire of imagery, incorporating Nilotic, agricultural, and pastoral, and mythological representations, all testifying to a developed classical comprehension, both literary and cultural.

The town of Madaba is renowned for both the quality and the quantity of its mosaics. An important center for mosaic production

▼ **The attendants of the Empress Theodora, San Vitale, Ravenna, Italy, mid-sixth century AD.**

The figures are highly decorated, front-facing, and seem to live in an unreal realm. They are seen as exquisitely ornate objects, with only the merest hints of portraiture visible in the first two attendants, while the remaining five form a beautifully balanced composition in the Imperial hierarchy. Though richly adorned, there is no attempt in the composition to achieve an illusion of depth or to create bodily substance. Abstract qualities are observed and delighted in. The color palette is harmoniously balanced with contrasting reds and greens enriched with white, gold, and purple. The border uses discs of mother-of-pearl to create a jeweled architectural frame. Glass is used to enhance these qualities in yet another way. Each tessera is angled directly into the mortar to catch the light and disperse it over the surface for greatest effect, constructing in the church an interior that glistens with myriad cubes of light and lustrous color.

during Imperial times, it is rich in mosaics of classical erudition. The decoration of an irregular-shaped room known as the Hippolytus Hall is remarkable in its completeness and its beauty. The design was probably based on a Hellenistic cartoon but has been translated into mosaic with a thorough understanding of design and coloring.

We know who the characters are in the Hippolytus Hall mosaic from the writing above each personage. Jordanian mosaics are characterized by numerous inscriptions that are incorporated into the floor designs as part of the overall decorative scheme. This symbiosis was to be developed to a fine degree in the decoration of the Islamic period and beyond.

In Israel, as in Syria and Jordan, mosaic floors were conceived as a single artistic unit subdivided into areas connected by loops of intertwining geometry or by vine and foliate tendrils framing the various subsections. Outer borders were densely depicted with acanthus scrolling or other richly elaborate framing, which often contained motifs from a hunting or mythological tradition.

The choice of subject matter was gradually influenced by theological conceptions, both from the church and, in Palestine (Israel), from the synagogue. Over one thousand mosaics have been found in the Holy Land. The presence of synagogue decorations attests to the existence of a flourishing Jewish community during the Byzantine period.

In the West, the art of late antiquity and early Byzantium spread as far as Aix-la-Chapelle/Aachen (Germany) and Saint Germigny-des-Près (France). However, it was in Italy, and particularly in Rome, where there was a continuing mosaic development. In the mosaic in the apse of the sixth-century church of Saints Cosma and Damiano in Rome, the abstract qualities of color in mosaic that are seen in Ravenna of the same period are remarkably revealed. The standing figure of Christ, centrally placed within the curvature of the apse, appears to hover majestically in space surrounded by a host of linear clouds. The clouds are primarily of red, red/blue, and blue glass tesserae. The red tesserae advance their presence and the blue tesserae recede, thus creating an oscillatory spatial sense on which the figure is placed. This chromatic resonance was not to be fully explored

again in all its abstract power and simplicity until the twentieth century. The mosaicists of the early Byzantine period were fully aware of the qualities inherent in the materials with which they worked.

In the little chapel of St Zenone in Santa Prassede in Rome there exists what has been termed "Il Giardino del Paradiso," the Garden of Paradise. The inside of the chapel is covered with gold and smalti to create a glowing chromatic interior which delights in the medium's capacity to create a space of mystery, wonderment, and spiritual remoteness. Even the windows are framed with glittering abstract ornament. The imagery is that of accepted religious hierarchy but realized with exquisite decorative splendor.

▲ **The Hippolytus Hall, Madaba, Jordan, sixth century AD.**
The mosaic covers the floor as a richly conceived carpet. The story of the Euripidean drama of Hippolytus and Phaedra is divided into rectangular registers. These are surrounded by a border of acanthus scrolls containing pastoral and hunting scenes. There are four personifications of the seasons, represented as Tyches, goddesses of Fortune, one in each corner. The remaining area to the wall has pairs of marine animals and birds recalling the imagery of the Nile. There is also a threshold mosaic of a pair of sandals in a roundel. The upper panel shows Aphrodite sitting next to Adonis; she is holding a slipper with which she is evidently about to chastise a winged cupid.

▲ **Zodiac (detail), Beth Alpha synagogue, Israel, sixth century** AD.
One of four mosaics containing zodiac signs, in a synagogue pavement. The mosaic was not worked on by a Greek mosaicist but by a father and son, as can be deciphered in an inscription worked into the pavement. It is a lively and naïve depiction immersed in a pagan Roman tradition. Apollo, the sun god, is centrally depicted and haloed, as were later depictions of Christ.

In the middle of the eighth century one member of the Umayyad family escaped massacres in Syria to found a new Umayyad Emirate, the Caliphate in Spain. Power and influence were demonstrated in the construction of new buildings. Under the Caliphate rulers a branch of art known as Hispano/Moresque flourished in Andalusia, based at Cordoba , the capital city. In the middle of the tenth century, under the ruler Al-Hakam II, a new *mihrab* (or niche, indicating the direction of Mecca) was added to the Great Mosque at Cordoba. It is a deep niche, shimmering with gold mosaic and overlaid with mystic undertones. Its Byzantine character is apparent in the use of gold and colored smalti, and although initial work was carried out with Byzantine expertise, one difference is immediately apparent: the tesserae are laid flat to emphasize the intricacy of decorative design in a two-dimensional manner and are not angled, as in Constantinople, Ravenna, and the great European Byzantine centers.

▼ **Detail from the Umayyad Mosque, the Treasury, Damascus, Syria, eighth century** AD. *The decoration represents ornamentally developed trees and stylistically developed architecture. The imagery appears idyllic, perhaps signifying an Islamic Golden Age.*

In the Near East the art of mosaic was adopted by the new Muslim rulers to decorate their mosques and places of worship. Early in the seventh century AD, Muhammad, the messenger of Allah, had received his divine call to instigate a new moral theory – Islam. In 661 the Arab/Muslim capital moved from ancient Medina to Damascus in Syria and a unifying dynasty was created to rule the empire until AD 750. These were the Umayyads, originally an aristocratic family of Mecca.
Two great buildings which utilized mosaic to proclaim the new religion within a lavishly rich setting arose from this period: the Dome of the Rock in Jerusalem and the Great Mosque at Damascus. Both are sumptuously decorative, with nonfigurative designs which show a strongly Byzantine influence. The imagery is rich with trees, fruit, acanthus leaves, and scrolls, and the materials are of smalti, gold smalti, mother-of-pearl, and semiprecious stones. The overall effect is Byzantine but included is imagery from the pre-Islamic art of Syria and Iran, for example an elegant tulip-like flower-bud design.

▲ **The Dome of the Chapel of Saint Zenone, Santa Prassede, Rome, Italy, ninth century** AD. *The shallow vault stands on four granite columns and these sustain four angels who are supporting a* tondo, *or roundel, of Christ. Their cheeks and hair are highlighted in bright orange hues and a warm golden patina that glows to maximum effect against the complementary blue of their halos. The effect is masterly.*

middle and late byzantine

The Middle Byzantine period in mosaic stretches approximately from the tenth to the thirteenth centuries.

The Arab, Byzantine, and Roman elements present in twelfth-century Sicily were fused together to produce some outstanding monuments. Although not so apparent in the glittering and refined monuments of the Palatine chapel, the Cathedral of Cefalù and the little Martorana church, they are harmoniously intermingled in the Cathedral of Monreale, a true masterpiece of Sicilian art.

The Arab tradition is seen in the white facing of marble and arabesque bands of mosaic, and stylized images of palms and plants. The Byzantine legacy is evident in the iconography, the mosaic dosserets on the capitals, and the covering of the whole interior with mosaic. Classic art imparts an order and uniformity to the grand design like a temple of old, and puts a certain humanity into the features of the many figures. The mosaic work completed in 10 years surely reflects the presence of one master mosaicist, a single mind with an overall vision, for it is known that Greek, Venetian, and local Sicilian artists were all working on the decoration.

The mosaic configuration of the cathedral illustrates a divine plan, the Creation, the disobedience of Adam and Eve in Paradise, and the salvation of the world, revealed in a system of registers of 130 panels and medallions. The interior of the cathedral is alive with gold and polychromatic glitter from its mosaic surface, and is the largest known composition, comprising 7,584 square yards (6,340 square meters) of mosaic. The vast golden expanse, like a rich covering of carpet, dematerializes the walls and gives the figures in still, stylized contemplation, a mysterious sparkling movement – such is the eloquence of the mosaic medium.

After the exuberance of the cathedral, it is in its cloister that an ethereal encounter of the simplest kind can be experienced. Built at the same time as the cathedral, the cloister is composed of 228 pairs of slender columns, surmounted by lively Romanesque capitals forming a multi-arched arcade. Some of the columns are plain and some are intricately carved, while others are inlaid with mosaic in gently spiraling strands or bands of geometric design. The mosaic inlay enlivens the architecture as a whole, and the play of light and shade in the portico increases the atmosphere of serenity and extreme beauty. This example of a genuine external delight from Western and Oriental derivation originates in Sicily. The polychrome mosaic inlays were inspirationally used on façades and in interiors throughout Italy in the succeeding centuries – a particularly beautiful and successful collaboration can be seen at Orvieto Cathedral in Tuscany.

The mosaics of St Mark's Basilica in Venice are in great part inspired by those of the Cathedral of Monreale in Sicily. Influence came also from further afield – from Greece and from Nordic/Germanic regions – as well as nearer by, from Tuscany and Ravenna. All conspire to make the interior one of the richest configurations of historic and sacred reference in the repertoire of church imagery. Apses, cupolas, atria, nave, and narthex – all conceivable surfaces (including a wonderful floor) pay homage to a great flowering of mosaic illustration.

▼ **A Byzantine Dosseret, Monreale Cathedral, Sicily, Italy, twelfth century** AD.
Each of the 18 granite columns on square bases has a capital from classical antiquity, some showing pagan deities. On the capitals rest 18 smooth dosserets, or blocks of stone, of Byzantine style and covered with mosaic decoration with central crosses. These dosserets support 18 piers, from which spring Arab-type arches supporting the walls of the nave.

Most memorable are the scenes of the dance of Salome from Herod's Feast in the fourteenth century baptistery, where the svelte figure of the dancer is portrayed in glorious red with pale white and blue fur sleeves and trimmings, a portent of the strong coloration that would be seen in Venetian oil paintings of later centuries. The atrium mosaics, densely encrusting the three shallow domes, likewise continue to amaze by their mastery of decorative composition.

late byzantine mosaic

Gold backgrounds played a dominant role in the vast expanses of vault and wall decoration throughout this period, but color, though of vivid intensity, relied heavily for its effect on pure single-color areas.

The folds in clothing and the detailing of architectural settings were articulated only by a strong linear technique, and highlights were outlined in single files of white tesserae.

In the fourteenth century there was a return to the glorious color blending of the early Byzantine period. Bold combinations of tesserae in different colors again came into play. This final flowering is sometimes termed the Paleological Renaissance. A splendid example of this reawakening is in Byzantium/Istanbul itself, at the monastery of Chora, now the Khariye museum. The figures show the childhood and life of Mary, the mother of Christ, and the ancestry of Christ, and the splendid domes are imbued with a new vivacity through the chromatic rendering of color.

◀ **The Genesis Dome, Atrium (detail), St Mark's Basilica, Venice, Italy, thirteenth century.**
The design consists of concentric narrative friezes telling of the creation of the world in the Old Testament, and the story of the Garden of Eden, above four six-winged angels realized in brilliant blue, red, and gold. The narrative clarity of the arrangement when viewed from below is staggering, and never ceases to delight and inform. The heavily fleshy figures of Adam and Eve outlined in a single line of red smalti show a marked Northern European influence and are easily seen against a luscious green and gold background.

renaissance decline
From the fifteenth century through to the early nineteenth century there was what has generally been acknowledged as a decline in mosaic artistry. The fully understood abstract nature and qualities of the medium, which relied heavily on the inherent constitution of the material, were to be presumptuously superseded by a painterly technique with qualities suited to the more fluid application of the brush than to the product of a hammer and chisel.

Nowhere was this more clearly demonstrated than in St Mark's in Venice. As many of the Byzantine mosaics began to deteriorate or became damaged in various ways – such as by fire, or even by cannon fire – they needed to be repaired. Painters of great renown, like Titian, Tintoretto, and Veronese, vied with each other to replace the "old-style" mosaics with new designs in a "modern" or High Renaissance style. A Venetian style developed, with Renaissance and Mannerist conceits, and the quintessential spirit of the earlier work was denied. As painters and a painterly style began to dominate, mosaicists were reduced to making mosaics look like paintings by introducing perspective, illusion, and plastic or sculptural qualities into the works. Many well-known paintings were scrupulously copied and the resulting mosaics put on public view to deceive or foil the viewer and to preserve the original. These were termed "paintings for eternity."

pre-columbian mexico
During the sixteenth century patrons and artists throughout Europe marveled at the artifacts coming to the West and the Court of King Charles V of Spain. These were the spoils taken by the Spanish Conquistadors from Mexico and Peru. Some of the treasures were of Aztec origin and were covered with precious stones and chalcedonies, particularly turquoise, rare shells, mother-of-pearl, and gold. The tiny, fashioned tesserae were irregularly shaped and tightly tessellated, forming a closely faceted skin of color and value.

The encrusted items were used in rituals and ceremonies, and were worn by priests and kings as symbols of their authority. Helmets, pectorals, masks, ritual shields, and headdresses to which spectacularly colored feathers were attached, made up some of the regalia.

▶ **Transfiguration, mosaic copy of a painting by Raphael, St Peter's, Rome, Italy, eighteenth century.**
The "painting" is made with hundreds of closely aligned tesserae in every nuance of color, after a painting by Raphael. The interstices that characterize mosaic are denied, the preference being for an imitation of a glossy, oil-painted surface.

This independent tradition of mosaic making had ancient roots in Peru and Mexico, dating from the first millennium BC, where precious inlaid objects were used in the realm of worship. It would seem that the skillful and unique nature of mosaic in supplying a decorative and significant finish to an object or structure has played an integral role in changing the ordinary into the extraordinary for many peoples of differing cultures and beliefs, thereby becoming a true reflection of the spirit of an age.

glassmaker, evolved a method known as the indirect or reverse technique of making up mosaics using manufactured glass with a smooth and regular surface and shape. In the workshops in Murano, and later in Venice, the tesserae were cut and temporarily applied face down onto a strong backing paper. These works, which could be of indeterminate size, were then carefully packed up and transported ready-made to wherever needed, and reassembled and fixed by workmen at their permanent site.

In England, Queen Victoria, who had recently lost her beloved husband, Prince Albert, erected a memorial extravaganza to his memory that is bedecked with mosaics from the workshop of Salviati. Many churches, private homes, and academies were decorated in this fashion – a cheaper and more efficient method of application, and equally quick to catch on in France, Germany, Eastern Europe, and beyond.

Much of the work, however, could appear lifeless, flat, and even pedantic, since the surface was generally flat and uniform without access to the wondrous light changes that occur on an uneven surface – properties that are inherent in hand-made and hand-cut smalti.

▼ **Casa Mila, 1906–1910; (detail), Antonio Gaudí, Barcelona, Spain.**
The roof terrace of the Casa Mila, colloquially known as La Predrera, is a veritable exhibition of surreal abstract "sculpture." Each ventilator for the apartment block is coated with tiles, mostly white, to create an extraordinary three-dimensional roofscape.

the victorians

The generally acknowledged artistic decline in mosaic technique in the West was halted by an upsurge in demand for large-scale architectural projects in the mid- to late nineteenth century after the pioneering of a technique of mosaic making in Venice which industrialized the method of production. Antonio Salviati, who was a lawyer, a motivator, and an entrepreneur, and Lorenzo Radi, who was a highly skilled Murano

▲ **St John (detail), Leeds Parish Church, England, 1876.**
One of 14 life-size figures made by the Venetian firm of Salviati and Co. Using the indirect method of setting, the mosaic depicts a rare and lively use of the method.

early and mid-twentieth century

One artist who was to use the indirect method to flourishing advantage was the Russian-born Boris Anrep (1883–1969). He executed many private and public commissions in England, including mosaic walls at Westminster Cathedral (1924, 1957–61), and the mosaic floors in the National Gallery (1927), the Bank of England (1927–37), and the Tate Gallery.

► Boris Anrep, Blake Room, Tate Gallery, London, England, 1923. Detail, floor mosaic.
Boris Anrep took proverbs from William Blake's poem "The Marriage of Heaven and Hell" to decorate the floor of one room in the Tate Gallery. The works were done in reverse technique and placed in position around a central heating vent. The proverb reads, "If the fool would persist in his folly he would become wise."

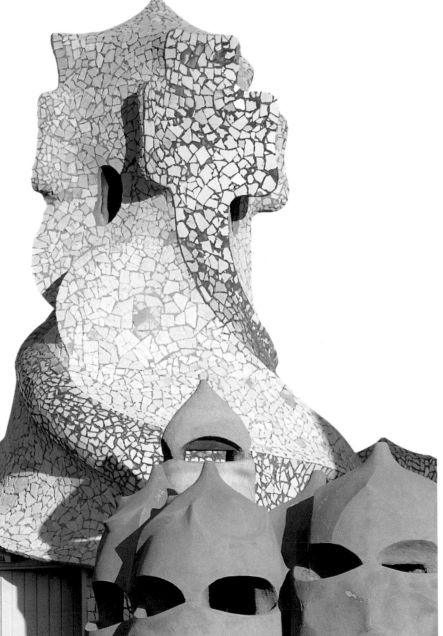

25

art nouveau

Only at the very end of the nineteenth century, with the advent of Art Nouveau, was a true vitality injected into the medium of mosaic. The nature of the Art Nouveau style, which is sometimes termed *Jugenstil*, or the Yellow Book style, and which gained popularity in the 1890s and early 1900s, is characterized by undulating lines and a marked decorative tendency. The Viennese artist Gustav Klimt was one exponent who, returning after a trip to Ravenna in 1903 to see and study the Byzantine mosaics, created a series of mural montages that incorporated mosaic, areas of painting, and specially commissioned ceramics. The effect is a glorious and elegant refinement of a purely personal technique that combined the exoticism of mosaic materials with the refined confines of an applied style.

One man of Spanish Catalan descent was to play a very influential investigative role in a new approach for mosaic. The progenitor of Art Nouveau, the artist/architect Antonio Gaudí, was to explore his interest with organic form and shape, not only of a two-dimensional nature but as an integral part of his architecture. Gaudí created a long series of projects and buildings, many of which were inspired by the Arab/Moresque tradition of Andalucia. From early on he made great decorative use of colored, glazed tiles on the façades of buildings. Under the patronage of the wealthiest Catalan, Count Güell, Gaudí developed a highly personal style in which mosaic came to feature prominently. Tiles were a cheap and indigenous material and Gaudí used them prolifically and innovatively to add color to his three-dimensional features such as roofing tiles, ventilation shafts, undulating park benches, and fountains. Unlike the internal mystery of a Byzantine church, suffused with color and light, Gaudí's world was external, fanciful, bold, and sculptural, aspects that had great appeal for the socialists of Mexico in the 1950s, and for an increasing band of Naïve explorers of the medium.

A third artist spanning the turn of the century who was also to have an enormous influence on mosaic making, particularly in Italy, was the Cubist/Futurist artist Gino Severini (1883–1966). His lifelong enthusiasm for and exploration of the techniques of mosaic within a painterly context – but with full understanding of the material, its light effects, and color resonance – are reflected in many delightful, small still-life mosaics carried out between 1930 and 1960. He initiated and founded two schools of mosaic – one in Paris, France, and the other in Ravenna, Italy – the Instituto Statale d'Arte per Mosaico "Gino Severini," or the Institute of Gino Severini, which continues to have an impressive line-up of teachers and students of great skill and originality.

During the mid-twentieth century a number of well-known artists worked with mosaic, at least in part, helping to explore and expand its boundaries within the context of the times. Diego Rivera, a social realist painter, and his associates in Latin America, Juan O'Gorman, Carlos Chávez Morado, David Alfaro Siqueiros, and others, were working within new critical and political values to promote a strong sense of national identity. They produced large-scale public murals and three-dimensional works that drew largely on their colorful historical past. Glazed and unglazed tiles were used alongside indigenous stones, providing a material that was a less expensive alternative to costly imported Italian smalti glass for covering large expanses within economic restrictions.

Other artists commissioned work to be turned into stone and glass, making "pictures for eternity" and thus perpetuating the concept of the seventeenth century but often with an innate understanding of how apt and attractive mosaic was in purveying abstract explorations or inquiries into color concepts. These include Pablo Picasso, Henri Matisse, Marc Chagall, and Fernand Leger.

One artist, working in London, had a complete understanding of the mosaic medium. Hans Unger, with his associate Eberhard Schulze,

created mosaics that explored the qualities of the medium and allowed their work to delight in the dynamics of the material. Surfaces were composed of large and small tesserae with raised and lowered surfaces, creating rhythmic tensions of color and shadow. Their compositions have a masterly control which often insists on the insertion of objects related to the individual work.

An American artist from New York, Jeanne Reynall, an apprentice student of Boris Anrep and contemporary of the abstract artist Jackson Pollock, took mosaic to an interesting extreme. Fragments of smalti glass were "dribbled" with a minimum of control onto colored grouts, often blue and pale pink or yellow, to create titles like "Remembrance" and "Reincarnation Lullaby." These abstract lyrical works show extraordinary sensitivity toward the mosaic material, for developing a very personal expression.

▼ **Penguin Books Ltd, Harmondsworth, London, England, Hans Unger and Eberhard Schultze, detail, 1964.**
Smalti of turquoise and green and orange, colors of the Penguin paperback series, resonate with tesserae of varying size, reflection, and intensity. The insertion of slate and polished typeface from the publishing company individualizes the mural and gives specific interest.

the naïves

Untutored artists, the Naïves, were also turning to mosaic for their self-expression, often in complete and happy ignorance of the "artistic scene" and motivated only by a desire to create. Most of these works are three-dimensional and large-scale, and have been made following an obsessional dream or ideal.

During the 1930s in France, Raymond Isidore (1900–1964), a gravedigger from St Chéron on the outskirts of Chartres, collected discarded glass and porcelain to decorate his modest house. Initially inspired by finding one glistening shard of blue glass, he continued to forage for the rest of his life to service his obsession – which was to encrust his whole environment with mosaic. His waking hours were spent in collecting miscellaneous refuse, garbage, and crockery to cover the beds, tables, clocks, flowerpots, walls, windows, floors, and ceilings. His designs were directed by his dreams, which furnished him with vivid images of his life and childhood, and also by illustrations from magazines and newspapers. "Picassiette," as he was affectionately termed, claimed divine intervention as his Muse and Inspiration.

One man of true and untutored genius is the Indian artist, Sri Nek Chand Saini (b. 1924). He works in Northern India, in Chandigarh, the city of the Swiss architect Le Corbusier. From 1958, while employed as a roads inspector, he began to work in complete secrecy, sometimes with his wife, to create a kingdom of rocks and industrial and urban rubbish, hidden from view behind disused tar barrels. Some 40 years later, the kingdom, which was motivated by a childhood dream, is now called the Rock Garden, and is internationally acclaimed, attracting visitors in numbers that make it the second most visited site in India after the Taj Mahal.

The imagery of the main garden is that of the whole of India – snake charmers, water collectors, goddesses, beggars, villagers, animals, drunkards – over 5,000 figures created from plain china, glittering bangles, eroded rocks, expired neon strip lights, porcelain electrical fittings, among much else. The armatures on which cement is added prior to the mosaic debris are also recycled – for example, the horns of buffaloes have been made from the handlebars of the ubiquitous bicycle seen all over India – and natural rocks resemble the most beauteous of female forms. The effect is stunning, humorous, awe-inspiring, humbling – it is a world of emotions. Work continues on an architectural phase, encompassing waterfalls, walkways, and gorges.

27

▶ **Courtyard wall, La Maison Picassiette, detail, Chartres, France, 1930s to 1980.** *The walls of the courtyard have life-sized mosaics, representing the artist, his wife and family, made from highly colored crockery. Flowers, birds, leaves, and butterflies crowd the walls in a riotous jumble of color and fragmentation. After his death his wife continued to maintain the garden.*

A kingdom of the possible in mosaic, it is an organic and wondrous inspiration, realized under the severe brow of the famed Secretariat building in Chandigarh, Le Corbusier's city of sectors and rationality. **The celebrated artist** Niki de Saint Phalle (b. 1930) was initially inspired to create her Tarot Garden, "Il Giardino dei Tarocchi," in Southern Tuscany in Italy by a visit at the age of 25 to Barcelona, to see the work of Antonio Gaudí in the Parc Güell. Her personal style of naïveté is more than just an homage – she has created a secret place revealed as a garden of mystery, magic, and potency with a radiance of color. It is, however, the artist's very singular experience, not a universally shared language.

The 22 sculptures are sculptural embodiments of the 22 Tarot cards, covered with skins of specially created materials – mirror glass, and ceramic and glazed tiles. The smaller sculptures, which include the Oracle, Death, and the Devil, have a polyester resin frame, while the larger central sculptures of the High Priestess, Sphinx, and Tower of Babel have iron armatures surrounded with wire meshing and a cement finish. Some of the works incorporate the sculptures of Jean Tinguely as both still and kinetic works. The extensive use of mirror in the outside garden situation creates spatial illusions, like the reflective surfaces of gold smalti in Byzantium, to dematerialize and perpetuate the private mystery of the garden and to exaggerate the ambiguity of age-old symbols.

▼ **Detail, the Rock Garden, Nek Chand Saini, Chandigarh, India, 1960s.**
A general view of one area from the first phase of this wondrous garden. It shows terraces of figures and animals, walls and ground, covered in utility china and encompassing all aspects of Indian life forms.

public mosaics

Public spaces and walls with their inviting empty expanses and unadorned surfaces have always lured artists committed to a cause or ideal to make works that would explain or expound their beliefs. These sculptures and murals have as their starting point some political or social ideal which, it is felt, should be voiced within a communal setting. This form of public art, often referred to as Community Art, is an art born of the city, and was prevalent from the 1970s and 1980s. Artists carrying out the work most often work in groups, bound by a single cause.

Mosaic is an ideal medium through which to meet this situation. By permanent fixing in cement, a durable weatherproof surface is created. The very fragmentary nature of this surface deters possible vandalism and graffiti within its urban setting and when completed the mosaic demands very little maintenance or upkeep, beyond an occasional clean or hosing.

In 1969 a London-based group known as Free Form was set up by Martin Goodrich and Barbara Wheeler-Early to create large-scale

▶ **The Emperor, detail, the Tarot Garden, Niki de Saint Phalle, Garavicchio, Tuscany, Italy, 1979–1996.**
The influence of Gaudí is observed most strongly in this work (Card no. IV) which encompasses a fountain, and a treelike arcade (compare with Parc Güell). Surmounting the structure is a tower, a-glitter with color and golden finials. The card in the pack represents male power and energy.

29

▶ **St Thomas Railway Arches "Pigeon Mural," detail, Elaine M. Goodwin and Group 5, 1991, Exeter, England.**
The under-bridge walkway had been dark and unsavory and home to myriad pigeons. Work was done to encourage the pigeons to roost away from the area. The Group put 91 of the pigeons back – as mosaic creations on the mural. The retired railway workers of the area "advised" on the creating of the mural and donated souvenir china and mementos. Local characters and dogs appear in the mural, as does a celebrated carrier pigeon, which won the Dicken Medal for bravery during World War II. The walkway is now lit and cleaned for people to use safely.

works in public spaces to improve the environment and bring benefits to the community in which it worked, and continues to do so. During the 1980s a mural known as the Easterhouse Mosaic, was made in one of the most deprived areas in the city of Glasgow in Scotland. Led by artists working with members of the community, the project helped both to provide a platform for local talent and to raise social issues within the area. The presence of the mural helped change the image of the district, and the slogan of those participating was "Where there is no vision people perish."

In 1985 in the city of Exeter in the southwest of England, a group was formed to work with the author to create public murals in mosaic. Called Group 5, they have to date created 14 murals, some in areas that previously lacked a strong identity and had attracted vandalism, and also in schools to provide a focus of color and interest. The materials were frequently recycled tiles, china, and miscellaneous articles given by the citizens and shopkeepers of Exeter and its locality. Each mural was unique to its site, sometimes establishing a

historical link, and sometimes drawing attention to its purpose, as on the façade of a community center. In each case its completion brought about improvements, whether practically through maintenance, lighting, security, and safety systems, as in each of the four parking-lot murals, or by adding color and life to formerly neglected and dreary structures, as in the City Walls mosaic.

In the Byzantine city of Ravenna in Italy during the 1980s a group of international mosaic artists created a "Park of Peace" – the Parco della Pace – to celebrate the theme in two- and three-dimensional works. Previously the area was an open urban space devoid of color and character. Artists from Russia, New Zealand, Italy, Belgium, America, Austria, and France were among those who took part in the project. Each artist contributed to the theme through stone, glass, rocks, and gold to make a group of monuments for public use and enjoyment. At the same time a link was established between Ravenna's glorious mosaic past and a vigorous expression for the future.

contemporary mosaic

Designers and craft workers are also turning increasingly toward mosaic to embellish the domestic, commercial, and industrial environment. Flourishing workshops exist in Italy, England, France, and Germany. In London the artists Emma Biggs and Tessa Hunkin of Mosaic Workshop, apart from repairing and restoring mosaics, use the medium to create colorful and exciting works for restaurants, interiors, and churches. Akomena in Ravenna, Italy, established in 1988 by Francesca Fabbri, is a workshop

▲ "Black and Grey Gold," 43 x 43 in/109 x 109 cm, by Lucio Orsoni, 1986.
The deceptively simple and pure lines of the mosaic lead the eye in an optical dance within a two-dimensional space. The colors, meticulously graded, control the dance in an exquisite observation – a mantra of form and illusion.

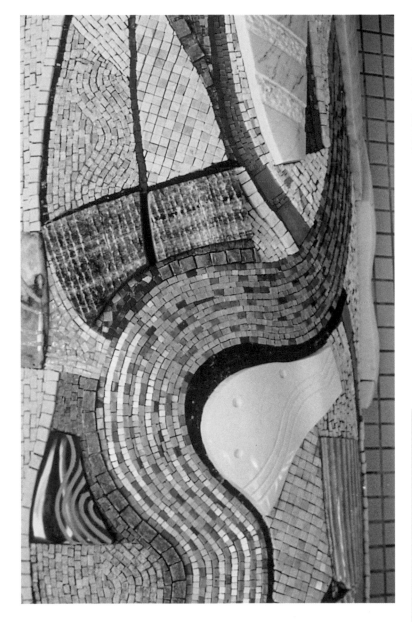

◀ The River – detail from a Public Mural entitled "Physical Balance" by Haruya Kudo, 1997 – underpass in Koriyama Station, Japan.
The work utilizes marble, smalti, gold, and silver, with elements of relief on five wall pillars. Eloquent areas of color and rhythmic design are set against a utilitarian background of simple white tiles uniformly laid.

devoted to finding contemporary uses for mosaic and experimenting with interpreting individual designs, many from notable artists.

Worldwide, artists are using mosaic for their self-expression: in Japan Haruya Kudo and Irie Tatsuya; in Norway Harriet Backer; in Egypt Muhammed Salem; in France Catherine Mandron, Verdiano Marzi, and Riccardo Licata; in Brazil Freda Jardim; in Israel Ilana Shafir; in Italy Marco de Luca, Felice Nittolo, Lucio Orsoni, Stefano Mazzotti, and Diego Esposito; in Canada Mireille Levesque; and in England Jane Muir and Maggy Howarth. These are just a few of the many excellent artists who are inspired by the material to find the perfect outlet for their expression. Mosaic when used with instinctive perception is unsurpassable as a medium in the creation of a work of infinite inspiration.

materials

A WIDE VARIETY OF MATERIALS CAN BE UTILIZED IN CREATING MOSAICS. THESE MAY INCLUDE PRECIOUS MATERIALS LIKE GOLD AND VENETIAN HAND-MADE GLASS, CALLED **SMALTI**, NATURAL MATERIALS LIKE STONE, PEBBLES, SHELL, AND MOTHER-OF-PEARL, AND MANUFACTURED OR RECYCLED MATERIALS LIKE CHINA AND TILE. WHATEVER THE MATERIAL CHOSEN, EACH COMES WITH UNIQUE PROPERTIES OF COLOR, TEXTURE, AND FINISH, AND EACH SHOULD BE USED EXPLOITATIVELY WITH SPECIAL REGARD TO THESE QUALITIES. BELOW IS A LIST OF MATERIALS MOST USED IN MOSAIC WORK FROM ITS ANCIENT BEGINNINGS UP TO THE PRESENT.

smalti For over 2,000 years glass has been used in the making of tesserae. The basic elements of glass are silica (usually sand) mixed with the flux (soda or potash) and compounds called stabilizers. To this mixture or batch are added coloring agents such as copper, chrome, and selenium. The mixture is then heated in a process called fusion, in which gases in the form of bubbles are eliminated and the solids are dissolved. This heating process may last days. The result is a viscous substance, a molten glass, which is poured onto a flat surface in the form of a disc ("pizza") or oblong slab, and cooled in a carefully controlled process called annealing. The resultant glass plate is then cut into tesserae by hand, using either a hammer and chisel or a semi-automated cutter. The variants of color, opacity, and brilliance have intrigued glassmakers throughout the long history of this amazing material, and many secrets or recipes are known and carefully guarded. **In its earliest use,** probably in the first century AD, the tesserae were generally of glass paste, not always opaque but more often semitranslucent. These can be seen, for example, in the Roman mosaics of Jordan. During Byzantine times, smalti in the red and yellow shades were produced with a higher lead content, which gave a more brilliant optical effect. During the fifteenth century, on the glassmaking island of Murano in the lagoon close to Venice, the glassmakers began to produce the material we know and love as smalti – an opaque material of intense coloring with a wonderfully brilliant reflective surface. This brilliance was obtained by greatly increasing the quantities of lead oxide. Another advantage of this addition was the greater

▲ **Smalti, showing imperfections, bubbles, colors, rounded edges.**

facility when cutting the material, since it is less brittle and therefore less prone to splintering.

Smalti is normally bought by the pound or kilo, in a color of one's choice. Sample colors are made available by each firm. Colors can be ordered to an exact shade but the cost would be greatly increased.

Smalti "pizze" can be bought whole, but usually the glass is bought already cut into a size approximating to just over and just under half an inch, or 15 × 10 mm. Any irregularities of size and color add interest to this exquisite mosaic material, and predetermine a lively surface whenever used.

▶ Part of the School of Mosaic color library in Spilimbergo, Friuli, Italy.

gold smalti (metal-leaf glass)

Gold has been used in mosaic work since the fourth century. It is a sumptuous material, which was used at its height in late Byzantine times when its qualities were understood in practical and spiritual terms.

▼ Gold smalti (metal-leaf glass).

smalti filati

These are threads or glass rods of smalti, used almost exclusively in the making of miniature or micromosaic. They were first used in the eighteenth century by the Studio of Mosaic at the Vatican to suit the tastes of the time, when mosaics were created to imitate oil paintings.

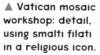

▲ Vatican mosaic workshop: detail, using smalti filati in a religious icon.

Gold tesserae are made up of a glass support base – these days transparent and colored yellow, green, or aquamarine, and ranging from around ¼–½ in/3–7 mm in thickness – and an upper protective layer of thin glass, the *cartellina* – which is generally clear but may be colored for producing colored golds. Interspersed between the two layers of glass is the metal leaf, a 24-carat gold, silver, copper, or alloy of gold and other metals. Sometimes the base is granulated to give a rippled finish, though generally the surface is smooth. Colors range from deepest gold to white, or may include blue, green, or pink – the color being made respectively by the cartellina, the metal, or the backing glass. A sample card of the golds produced today is obtainable, but they are subject to availability. At present there is only one firm in the world that produces this most exquisite, brilliant, and elusive of mosaic materials.

▲ Gold smalti – colored.

▲ Vitreous glass; various shades and surfaces.

▼ Ceramic mosaic tiles; various shades; glazed and unglazed; and mottled.

vitreous glass
This is the most commonly available mosaic glass and has the advantage of being cheaper than smalti. It is a standardized mosaic glass, used industrially, and is generally bought by the sheet (12 × 12 in/30 × 30 cm). Being a manufactured glass, vitreous glass is regular in format – normally about ¾ × ¾ in/2 × 2 cm – with a smooth upper edge, sloping shallow sides and a generally roughened bottom edge. The smooth side is used whenever a completely even surface is required. However, the roughened surface can be used for textured effects. Among the wide variety of colors and finishes that characterize vitreous glass are the brilliant imperial primary hues, the milky opaque colors, and finishes that are grainy or have a coppery iridescence.

ceramic mosaic tiles
Clay has been used in mosaic since ancient times in the form of terracotta tiles, glazed Samian ware, and bricks. Today clay tesserae can be bought glazed and unglazed. In the unglazed tile, the color is uniform throughout, while in the glazed tile, the glaze is superficial. They are readily available and inexpensive to purchase. Characteristically, their colors are earth colors, and they can be used whenever a Greco-Roman type of palette is needed and when marble is hard to acquire.

household tiles

Both new and used tiles with the backing plaster removed are a useful source of mosaic material. The glazes are often exciting and colorful. Large pieces of tile interspersed with smaller pieces add an interesting variant when you are covering large areas with mosaic. Take care not to use tiles with transfers – often found on the most modern of tiles – instead of real glazing effects.

▲ Household tiles; various.

china

China and crockery are some of the most exciting materials used in mosaic. There is an inexhaustible supply – both new and used, and broken. The nature of china is similar to that of smalti. The glazed curved areas give off a scintillating reflective surface that is not unlike the effects seen in Byzantine mosaic work. Richly bordered tableware, cup handles, and lids, all give an amusing and lively surface.

▼ China; various.

marble

Marble is a naturally occurring rock which has a crystalline appearance when cut. The colors are generally soft and muted but can be polished to provide more intense shades. It is generally cut with a marble hardie and hammer from rods into tesserae. Marble and stone of varying colors were traditionally used in Greco-Roman mosaics. Sometimes the stone was unique to the area and country in which the mosaics were made, although much marble was imported, especially from Egypt.

Colors range from white, chalky, pinks, rose, and ochers, to greens, blues, grays, and blacks.

▲ Tin Lane Community Center, Mosaic Mural, detail, Elaine M. Goodwin and Group 5, Exeter, England, 1988.
The mosaic is made of recycled materials – particularly china and tiles. The imagery depicts the internal activities of the center: youth club, toddler group, music group, women's group, and so on.

▼ Marble; various.

pebbles

River or sea pebbles are an easily obtainable material for mosaic use. They can be black, white, or polychrome. When collecting pebbles be sure to wash them to get rid of any salts. Sort and grade pebbles into color, shape, and size: this will be of great assistance when using them. Some of the earliest floor mosaics dating back to the eighth century BC and the fourth century BC were of pebbles, used in both naïve and highly sophisticated designs, for example at Olynthus, Pella, and Eretria.

Pebbles are best sealed after cleaning, using a sealer, which allows the color to remain natural and strong as if wet, yet without a varnished, polished look.

▶ **Pebbles; various.**

shells and mother-of-pearl

Shells have been used in mosaic since Roman times, having featured especially in grottoes and nymphaea where the connection with the sea is strong. There are good examples in Pompeii and Herculaneum. Shells can be used whole and pressed directly into the mortar, taking care first to fill the concave area of the shells with mortar to prevent any gaps that might render them fragile.

Mother-of-pearl is found on the inner surface of some shells, particularly the pearl oyster. When cut into shapes, using a band saw to cut through the calcium carbonate layers, it can be fixed like glass or ceramic into mortar. It has a soft, iridescent, and sometimes golden sheen. It was used in the sixth century AD in Ravenna to give a jewel-like appearance in the headdress of the Empress Theodora in the church of San Vitale, and in the cross on the apse mosaic at St Apollinare in Classe, Italy.

▶ **Shells, mother of pearl; various.**

miscellaneous

In addition to the more traditional materials used in the making of mosaics, other materials can be used for their specific values and properties. Any material used in mosaic must always be used judiciously, and the quality of each understood. In this way the resultant mosaic will have its own value and strength and will become more than just a pleasing surface.

Such materials can include slate, quartz, granite, lapis lazuli, turquoise, mirror, glass globules, semiprecious stones, bone, alabaster, and many more.

▶ **Miscellaneous; various, including granite, bone, agate, fool's gold, slate, glass, alabaster.**

equipment

IT IS ADVISABLE AT ALL TIMES TO OBSERVE THE HIGHEST STANDARDS OF SAFETY AND SECURITY. EXTREME CARE SHOULD BE TAKEN IN STORING FLAMMABLE AND POISONOUS MATERIALS. EYE SHIELDS AND DUST MASKS SHOULD BE WORN WHEN CUTTING MOSAIC MATERIALS, AND PROTECTIVE GLOVES WORN WHENEVER GROUTING AND CLEANING. EVERY POSSIBLE CARE SHOULD BE TAKEN IN ARRANGING THE STUDIO TO AVOID POSSIBLE MISHAPS AND ACCIDENTS. WHEN IN DOUBT WEAR PROTECTIVE CLOTHING AT ALL TIMES. READ AND OBEY ANY INSTRUCTIONS ON BOUGHT OR MANUFACTURED PRODUCTS. IF OCCASIONAL SPLINTERS OF GLASS CAUSE BLEEDING, HAVE EMERGENCY FIRST-AID KITS TO HAND OR SEEK MEDICAL ADVICE.

the studio/workspace

Mosaic is a medium that demands space – space for drawing, storing, working, and grouting. It also benefits from an adaptable space, for example in which to pin up drawings or spread out work on the floor or worktop. With good organization all can be arranged.

storing

The walls need sturdy shelving to support the materials, whether displayed in jars, cartons, or boxes. Storage containers should be color-coded and material-coded. This helps greatly in deciding a color palette and material for each work.

Tools should be kept dry to avoid rusting, and stored together in boxes or drawers for easy use.

Adhesives, cements, and grouts should be kept in a separate area, perhaps on a low shelf, and should avoid contact with any form of damp condition.

the floor

This needs to be easily kept clean or swept. Ideally this area should be uncluttered and adaptable to adjust to different sizes of work. Mosaic tesserae get everywhere! Slivers of ceramic and mosaic glass can find their way into every crevice, including clothing or even cups of coffee. Be aware! It is good practice to clean up after every day's work, and thoroughly at the end of each piece of mosaic work. Working with mosaic is dusty, so use windows or extractors to air the room. Dust must be kept to a minimum by observing simple procedures of cleaning up.

▲ **Materials storage.**

the workbench/worktop

If possible arrange to have at least two areas for working on. One area should be clean and have a flat surface with enough room to contain the drawing implements. It should be large enough to work at comfortably and at a height to maintain a good posture. It is advisable to be aware of not sitting or standing up for long periods of time – engrossed in the work! – and holding an unnatural or uncomfortable position. Develop an awareness of your posture. Arrange the working height to take account of this by fixing comfortable heights in the relationship of your stool or chair to the work top. Take frequent breaks for relaxing and changing your position. An angled board or worktop could greatly aid the working position.

A second area for cutting and making the mosaic is advantageous, since cements and glues can be messy. There also needs to be room for the materials to be near at hand while you are working.

▼ Keep a good posture at the workbench.

lighting

Natural lighting is always an advantage and a delight in many art procedures, and large windows or skylights are ideal. When dark, or if windows are inadequate, daylight bulbs are excellent for keeping colors true and giving a greater degree of natural light than normal tungsten bulbs. Good lighting and adequately directed lighting are of prime importance.

access to water

It is useful but not absolutely necessary to have water and a sink in the studio or workroom. Some internal area with water is required for mixing cements and grouts. Many artists prefer to grout outside and certainly an external area for cleaning mosaics is essential. Be careful at all times not to allow the cement to get into the water-pipe system through the drains – complete blockages can occur. Wrap any unused cement in newspaper or plastic and put it in the garbage can.

adhesives
A variety of adhesives is used in mosaic making, both traditional and modern. All are easily purchased at builders' yards and hardware stores. It is essential that the cements be stored in dry conditions, and that safety and protective measures be observed at all times.

water-based gum

This is a simple water-based adhesive which is easy to use. It is often called gum arabic or gum mucilage. It is suitable for sticking mosaic materials onto paper or cardboard. This is used in the reverse technique where material is temporarily glued to a paper backing and is easily washed off later with water.

white household glue

White household glue can be used as an adhesive on its own, or as a binder with other materials. It will bond together all mosaic materials including glass, ceramic, marble, stone, and wood – whenever there is at least one porous material. Interior and exterior grades can be bought. The exterior grade is waterproof when mixed with cement. White household glue can be used with sand and brick or marble dust to produce a textured setting bed. It can be mixed with cement to provide a strong malleable adhesive which can be built up sculpturally. It can also be diluted with water and used as a sealer for priming wood. It dries without color – a great advantage.

epoxy resin

This is a high-strength adhesive consisting of two separate components – the resin and the hardener. When mixed together in equal proportions, an extremely strong waterproof adhesive is formed with a limited workable time dependent on atmospheric conditions. Resin may be colored with pigment or textured with a variety of sands. It is excellent where mosaic will be permanently sited underwater, or used in damp conditions. It can be cleaned off with polyester solvent.

cement

The most widely used and traditional adhesive is cement. Portland cement is the most common and easily obtainable; its name is derived from the color of Portland stone in England. It has excellent adhesive qualities and can harden even underwater. It is a neutral gray color ideally suited for bedding and grouting mosaics. Its disadvantages are its weight – it is very heavy when used in mosaics of over three feet (one meter) – and it has a fairly short shelf life once opened; it should always maintain a silky feel.

Cement can be colored using cement pigments that come in a number of earth colors including brick red, moss green, ochers, and black. A white cement can also be obtained to which color can be added for a brighter finish.

Cement is normally used mixed with sand into a mortar for best adhesive properties and strength. The sand should be washed and not contain any salts.

There is much latitude in choosing proportions of sand to cement, and mosaicists often have their favorite recipes. Generally the proportions are in the ratio of three or four quantities of sand to one quantity of cement.

Lime in the form of hydrated lime is often added to the cement-and-sand mixture to retard its setting time and to give a more malleable mix which has less of a tendency to shrink and is therefore less likely to crack. Hydrated lime can be made by mixing lime and water to a smooth paste in a plastic container and leaving it for a few days to allow the surplus water to rise to the top. This is then poured away and a white doughy mixture is left. This can be added to the sand– cement mix in the same proportion as the cement. Should the hydrated lime dry out, never add more water: simply use the dried crumbly mixture in the same proportion. Alternatively a cement retarder – called a mortar plasticizer – can be bought from the builders' yard.

The advantages of preparing a personal mix are many. It is unique and the texture is controlled by the choice of sand. It is also much cheaper than a ready-made cement adhesive, which is an advantage if working within a restricted budget or on a very large scale.

Cement tile adhesives in which the sand (usually of a fine grade) is already included, can be bought. Water is then added as required, as well as a cement color pigment if necessary. Always make sure there is a cement base to the bought product, as many ordinary domestic tile cements have a limited bonding life. They are also much more difficult to clean than traditional cement–sand mortars.

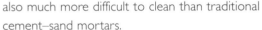

▼ **Various sands:
red, yellow, silver.**

tools

Each mosaic studio or workshop collects a miscellany of tools. Many are common to all but some are a selection unique to the individual mosaicist and reveal the peculiarly acquisitive nature of the mosaicist in the pursuit of his/her art. The basic tools, however, are listed below.

The hammer and hardie A traditional and essential tool for cutting marble, stone, and smalti glass. The **hammer** has a wooden handle and a steel head which is slightly curved at the top and has two cutting edges made from tungsten carbide. It can be of various weights, but in general is approximately two pounds – under one kilogram. The **hardie** is an inverted chisel, normally with a curved cutting edge that is also made of tungsten carbide. It is embedded in a wooden block or log cut to a comfortable height for use.

Mosaic nippers These are also made with tungsten carbide cutting edges for sharpness and for long-lasting use. They contain a spring, which greatly assists in the cutting technique, as the jaw is always open and ready to receive the mosaic material.

Other cutting tools include **glass cutters** for cutting stained glass and mirror, and **wire snips** and **pliers** for cutting wire mesh and steel line wire. **Studio knives** or **craft knives** and **scissors** are used for cutting card, paper, and fiber netting. They should be sharp for clean and efficient use.

◀ **Cutting tools**

1. mosaic hammer
2. scissor type pincers
3. mosaic tile nippers
4. craft knife
5. craft knife blades
6. glass cutter
7. scissors
8. tile scorer and cutter
9. pliers
10. knife
11. hardie
12. tin snips

▶ For spreading, making and cleaning

1. soft work top brush
2. dental prodders
3. dental tweezers
4. palette knife
5. soft hand brush
6. masonry brush
7. chisel
8. hammer
9. household brushes
10. paint brushes
11. adhesive/glue spreader
12. cement spreader
13. toothbrush

▶ For drawing and designing

1. 360° protractor
2. 180° protractor
3. set square
4. ruler
5. felt-tip pens
6. drawing pen
7. carbon paper
8. graph paper
9. drawing paper
10. steel rule
11. compasses
12. eraser
13. boxed eraser
14. pencils
15. T-square

other tools

Palette knife, spatulas, spreaders, tweezers,
dental instruments, hammer and chisel,
masonry brush, toothbrush, paint brushes,
glue brushes, sweeping brushes, surface
cleaning brush for scrap.

Pens, felt-tip pens, pencils, erasers, card,
paper, tracing paper, carbon paper, squared
paper, protractor, compasses, set squares,
T-square, ruler.

Brown paper, card, wood, fiber netting,
utensils of terracotta, wire mesh, line wire,
gauze or scrim, polyethylene sheeting.

Eye shields or goggles, dust masks, gloves.

Buckets, bowls, trowels, squeegee, level,
cloths, polyethylene sheeting, notched trowel,
water container.

Saw, drill, wall plugs, screws, countersink,
screwdrivers, screw eyes, panel pins, wire,
nylon thread, hammer, varnish and brush,
picture hooks, sandpaper, gimlet/awl, rust-
resist staples.

▲ For bases to
work on.

1. steel wire loop
2. plywood
3. brown paper
4. fiber netting
5. polyethylene
   sheeting
6. terracotta pot
7. roll of
   scrim/gauze
8. wire mesh
9. card

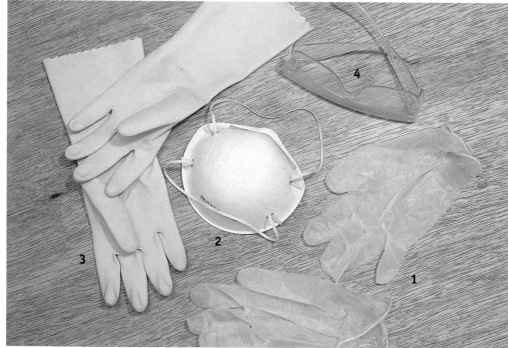

◄ For protection.

1. vinyl gloves
2. air filter
3. rubber gloves
4. goggles/eye
   protectors

► For framing and
hanging.

1. hammer
2. small brush
3. varnish
4. saw
5. screwdriver
6. awl/gimlet
7. countersink
8. drill
9. drill bit
10. sand/glass
    paper
11. staples
12. pliers
13. screw eyes
14. brass pins
15. picture hook
    and pins
16. screws
17. wall plugs
18. nylon wire
19. hanging wire

design

THE DESIGN MUST INITIALLY CORRESPOND WITH THE PURPOSE OF THE MOSAIC: WHETHER IT IS FOR PERSONAL OR FOR EXHIBITION PURPOSES OR FOR DOMESTIC OR PUBLIC DISPLAY. CONDITIONS SUCH AS SIZE, SITING, COLOR, LIGHTING, AND VIEWING POSITION MUST ALL BE TAKEN INTO CONSIDERATION. ONCE THESE ARE ASCERTAINED IT IS NECESSARY TO DESIGN THE MOSAIC WITH PARTICULAR REFERENCE TO THE MATERIALS USED AND TO THE DIRECT OR INDIRECT METHOD CHOSEN. THE IMAGE THEN HAS TO BE DETERMINED: ABSTRACT, GEOMETRIC, PICTORIAL, FIGURATIVE, SYMBOLIC. ONCE THIS IS DECIDED THE MOST CRUCIAL FACTOR IN CREATING A SUCCESSFUL MOSAIC IS THE INTERRELATIONSHIP BETWEEN THE DESIGN AND THE PLACING OF THE MATERIALS.

imagery

Nature is a great supplier of imagery for mosaic making. Birds, fish, reptiles, animals, figures, leaves, fruit, flowers, buds, trees, the sky, the sea, the land – all are perennial images which have been used in all cultures throughout time. A visit to a museum or a glance at an image in a book will develop an understanding of these images as symbols for continual exploration and understanding of the world in which we live.

Cities provide strong imagery through architecture, industrial sites, transport, machinery, signs, and logos.

Mood translates well into abstract mosaic using black and white or color, or an interaction of rhythm and tension in the direction of the tesserae. Feelings of calm, energy, turbulence, reflection, joy, despair, hope, and desire are some of the moods that can be translated through the material.

Geometry and shapes can produce intriguing mosaics, with circles, spirals, squares, lines, dots, checkers, Greek key patterns, and bar codes. Used singly or repetitively in patterns or as an underlying structure or symbol, geometric forms give strength to an image or border design.

Whatever imagery is chosen, it should have a real meaning for the creator. In this way it gains a motivation for its existence and becomes a well-grounded creation from which to build.

▶ Materials are chosen for color, texture, and size.

cartoon

For the mosaicist the cartoon is a preliminary sketch only. It can be of the simplest kind – a few strong lines and directional or color indications. Highly detailed drawings can hold back the natural progression of creating a mosaic piece by piece. Let the work itself dictate the direction of the mosaic – don't become a slave to the initial sketch. Simple drawings may be made directly onto the base in pencil and firmed up in pen: the thickness of a felt-tip pen corresponds more truly to the thickness of a mosaic material. More detailed cartoons made on paper can be transferred to wooden and terracotta bases using carbon paper or tracing paper, and enlarged or reduced by using a squaring-up procedure or photocopier.

▲ A full-size cartoon translated into a mosaic on fiber netting.

Designs can be transferred to cement, section by section, or by obtaining large photocopies, by squaring up, or by eye, and also by pricking through the design onto a rendered surface. In this case, as each section gets covered up by a layer of mortar, use registration marks made with a knife to help with the drawing. This is the way mosaics are known to have been created on walls from the fourth century onward.

A certain amount of spontaneity results in a livelier mosaic which inspires interest. A laborious work can appear just that, when it is completed.

color
Mosaic materials such as vitreous glass, china, glazed tiles, and smalti have infinite shades of color and hue. These can be mixed only on the mosaic surface itself and by the eye of the viewer when seen from a distance.

If large areas of the same color are to be used, vary the tones, sizes, even the materials, to add interest and to give intensity by setting up color vibration. Beautiful gradations of color can be built up by varying the shapes of the tesserae to bleed into each other to give exciting resonances. In areas of brown, green, and orange, juxtapose green and red, blue and yellow, and red and yellow respectively. Set opposing colors together for maximum intensity – purple with yellow, blue with orange, red with green. Outline areas in black or charcoal gray to heighten and separate color like stained-glass windows.

It is Important that, whatever image is decided upon, it must be of significance to the maker, who should feel free to explore and develop its potential fully, within the widely varied confines of the mosaic medium. Always keep in mind that a mosaic tessera is a unit of color, size, form, and finish – characteristics that are integral and special to each other and which, when joined one to another and another and another ... can create a living image unique in time and place.

49

◀ **Red square.**
*Various tesserae of red tones
are used to create a surface
of lively interest.*

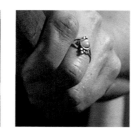

cutting and laying techniques

A NUMBER OF SPECIALIST TOOLS ARE USED IN MOSAIC MAKING TO CUT THE MATERIALS AVAILABLE TO THE MOSAIC ARTIST. IF FROM THE OUTSET THE CUTTING TECHNIQUES ARE FULLY UNDERSTOOD AND THE TOOLS ARE HANDLED CORRECTLY, ALL THE MATERIALS USED IN THE PROJECTS SHOULD BE CUT WITH FACILITY AND UNDER THE CONTROL OF THE ARTIST. IT IS, HOWEVER, ADVISABLE TO WEAR PROTECTIVE EYE SHIELDS AND DUST MASKS AT ALL TIMES, AND GLOVES WHEN CUTTING MIRROR AND GLASS.

hammer and hardie

The hardie should be at a convenient height for comfortable standing or sitting. If you're sitting, the hardie should be gripped between the knees. The traditional cutting tool for mosaicists, the hammer, is held in the cutting hand firmly but with a relaxed arm to enable the downward swinging action onto the hardie or chisel. Each blow should come from above and should aim to align the hammer with the chisel tip. Hold the tessera – normally marble, stone, or smalti – centrally on the chisel tip between the thumb and forefinger and swing the hammer down onto this point. With practice extremely accurate cutting is obtained and a rhythm built up between cutting and placing the tesserae. Persevere!

mosaic nippers

Mosaic nippers are a modern cutting tool which can be used to cut most materials, including vitreous glass, ceramic, tiles, china, and smalti tesserae. Hold the legs of the nippers toward their ends in the palm of the cutting hand, with the rounded edge of the jaw facing inward. With the other hand introduce the tessera face upward between thumb and forefinger into the open jaw. The tessera need only be inserted up to ¼ in (6 mm). Squeeze the legs of the tool together with the cutting hand and simultaneously press the thumb and the forefinger together. In this way equal and opposing pressure is exerted,

allowing the fracture to be a straight cut. Angle the head of the nippers to give diagonal lines. Always remember to align the finger and thumb with the direction of the mosaic nippers' head.

▲ **Using the hammer and hardie.**

▲ Using mosaic nippers for glass and ceramic.

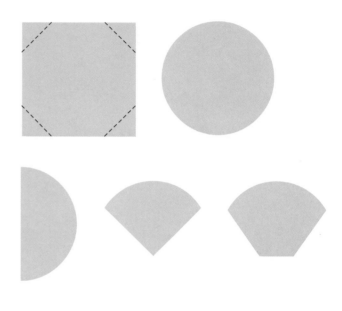

▲ Using mosaic nippers for large pieces of china and tile.

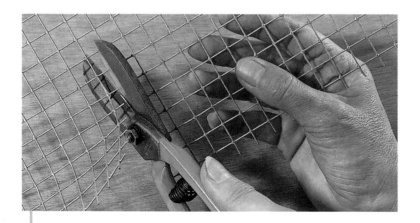

▲ The spring in this cutter enables wire and mesh to be cut with a scissor-like action.

Shapes that can be cut using the mosaic nipper:

Circles, semicircles, wedges.

With practice and a certain applied pressure, concave surfaces can be cut.

It helps if you can use a tile-cutting tool which you know will give exact sizes and clean, straight edges. There are a number of cutters on the market and all use the same principle of scoring and breaking. The most commonly used shapes. Quarters are the most often used; eighths are used as a running line for outlining and drawing.

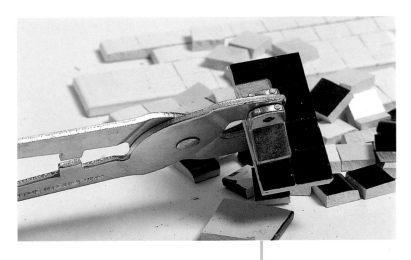

plier tile cutter
▲ Plier tile cutter

Place the tile on a flat surface and score its surface from one edge to the other with the small cutting wheel. Hold the tool in the cutting hand, center the flared anvil above the scoring line and squeeze the legs of the tile cutter gently together. The tile will break cleanly along the scored line.

glass cutter
▲ Glass cutter.

For cutting mirror or stained glass a simple glass cutter can prove invaluable. It is advisable to wear gloves when handling glass and mirror, since splintering can easily occur. Firmly but lightly score a line across the mirror using the tungsten-carbide wheel at the top. Gently use the ball of the cutter to tap the underside of the mirror — it will crack along this scored line.

laying techniques: *opus (opera)*

The ways in which mosaic tesserae are laid out or constructed are called the *Opus* (*opera* is the plural). A mosaic can be constructed using one or more of the methods and to a greater or lesser extent. There is a wide diversity and latitude in the laying of the material. Each mosaicist develops a personal style. By understanding the opus techniques, however, a deeper understanding of the placing of the materials is reached.

Opus Tessellatum

Used frequently in Roman times. The image is surrounded by one or two bands of tesserae to define its form. The background is constructed of more or less square tesserae in a fairly uniform horizontal or vertical linear pattern. Use of this method helps to stabilize an image within its surroundings.

Opus Vermiculatum

This is when the tesserae resemble vermicelli, or curved lines. It can be used within an image to give a feeling of movement or as a sinuous line. The term was used by scholars who described the fine detailing in the Greco-Roman emblemata as "little worms."

Opus Musivum

This occurs on larger floors when the smaller refined images of the emblemata are freed from their central position to become part of a large integrated floor creating an all-over design made in an architectural setting.

Opus Palladianum

The tesserae are cut into random shapes resembling a haphazardly laid paving. They can be tightly or loosely tessellated depending on the material and the required finish. It is an excellent method for use in backgrounds when you are left with asymmetrical, awkward, or irregular shapes.

Andamento

This is the way in which the tesserae are made to flow in directional lines. By being aware of the flow of the material, areas of rhythm and tension can be built up, contrasted, or exaggerated. The grouting lines can emphasize the flow by being of various widths and colors.

▼ **A la Recherche du Temps Perdu.**
A small panel adapting Opus Tessellatum *to give a strong horizontal 'landscape' ambience to the design of four trees.*

◄ **Abstract panel, showing *andamento*.**
An abstract panel emphasizing the wonderful movement and rhythm that can be built up by concentrating on the coursing of the tesserae with its accompanying grouting lines.

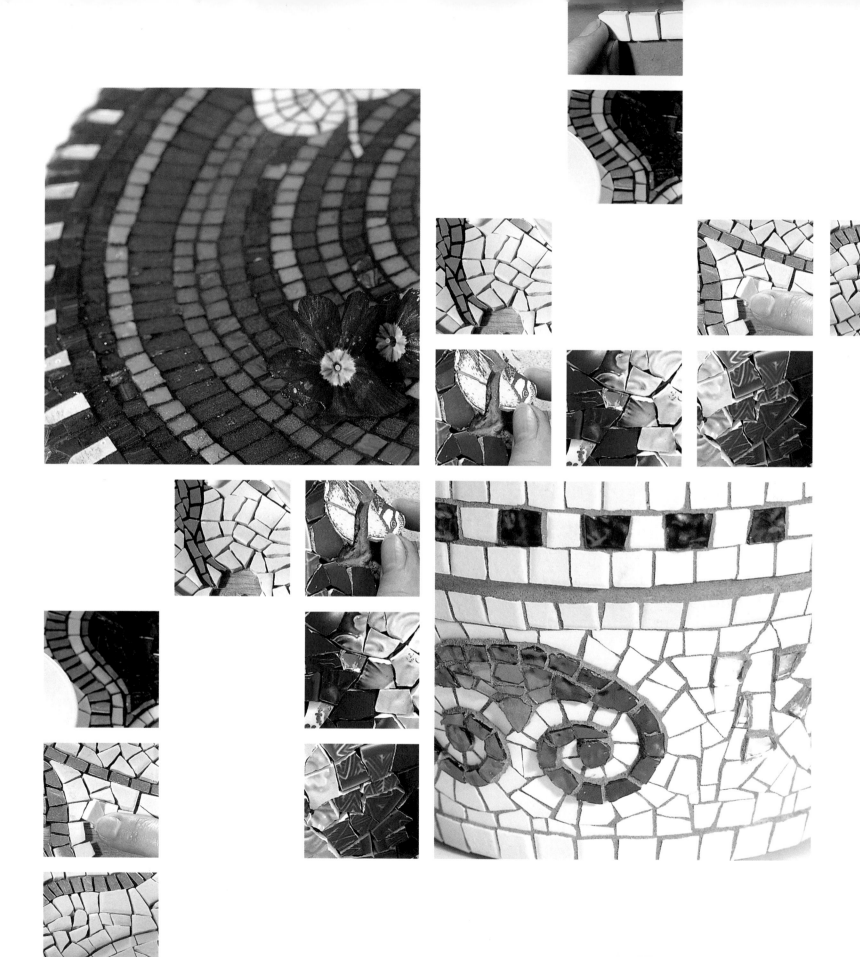

fixing techniques and bases

THERE ARE TWO MAIN METHODS OF MAKING MOSAICS TODAY – THE **DIRECT METHOD** AND THE **INDIRECT METHOD**.

THE DIRECT METHOD IS WHERE THE TESSERAE ARE FIXED FACE UPWARD ONTO THEIR BASE. THE **INDIRECT METHOD** IS WHERE THE TESSERAE ARE FIXED **TEMPORARILY**, FACE DOWNWARD, ONTO A BASE.

direct method

bases

In the early Sumerian mosaics the material was pressed directly onto a wooden base using a naturally occurring bitumen binder. In Roman times the setting bed was made from a mixture of volcanic ash, known as *pozzolana*, combined with lime. When mixed together with water, a strong cement was formed. Today mosaicists have a wide choice of materials on which to work into or onto, depending on the final position or destination of the mosaic.

wood

This is the most favored base for modern mosaicists, and is ideal for many situations. The wood is generally a plywood of internal or external quality, where the layers of wood are bonded to each other with a high-quality resin impermeable to water. It is easily sawn to the required shape and size, which should be portable. The edges can be sealed to provide a sure base for internal or protected external use as, for example, in a covered conservatory or porch. Plywood can never be one hundred percent waterproof. It is advisable to use plywood that is no less than ½ in/12 mm thick, to give a rigid support and to counteract any possible warping. The mosaic is made directly onto the wood and can be of any height and shape.

▼ **Table top (a).**
The tesserae are cut and a little white household glue applied on the back of each tessera.

▼ **Table top (b).**
The tesserae are then placed in position one after the other to tessellate the pieces carefully.

▼ **Table top (c).**
The table top uses ceramic, gold, and vitreous glass. The images combine Hindu, Christian, Islamic, and pagan motifs.

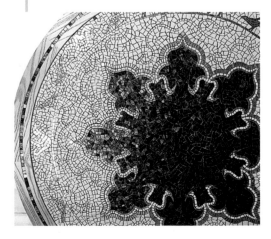

net

Netting is a fine-weaved resin fiber material which acts as a perfect base for an intermediary setting surface for mosaics before being transported to a permanent location. It can be cut to any shape or size and added to at will. It can be utilized wherever a mosaic is needed internally, or externally, on a wall, floor, or ceiling. **Generally the net** with its mosaic is embedded into cement for permanent fixing, or grouted before being fixed permanently with an epoxy resin glue. It can also be used, to a limited extent, to mold around gentle curves or indentations on a three-dimensional object.

▲ **Bird (a) drawing.**
The drawing is done on a sheet of white paper. The main lines are defined in black with a felt-tip pen.

▲ **Bird (b) fixing.**
The drawing is placed on a flat surface with a clear polyethylene sheet placed over it. The net is cut larger than the drawing, and put on top so that the drawing clearly shows through. The white household glue is applied in the direct way to the tesserae and onto the netting. The polyethylene sheet allows the finished mosaic to be lifted easily from the surface and turned over to dry thoroughly before being cut close to the outlined shape, for grouting.

▶ **Bird (c).**
The bird is made of ceramic, vitreous glass, and gold. The gold will glint in the daylight to brighten a shady courtyard wall.

▲ Flowerpot (a).
The tesserae are stuck to the terracotta frostproof base using an epoxy resin in a direct fixing method. The two-component glue has only a limited time to be used before hardening.

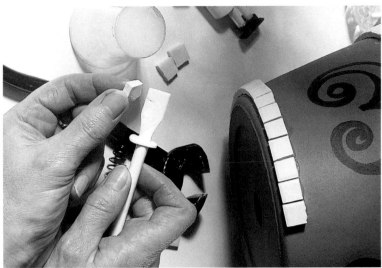

▲ Flowerpot (b).
It is best to fix small areas at a time. Because the epoxy is an impact glue, it will hold the tesserae in position on a vertical surface, but it must be used in a well-ventilated area. It is also advisable to make a test sample first to become familiar with the technique, and to have a quantity of tesserae precut for quicker and easier fixing.

terracotta

Portable terracotta trays or bases were used in Roman times on which to make finely detailed emblemata away from the main site. Today terracotta and clay utensils provide a versatile medium upon which to put mosaic. They can be hand-made and fired, or bought in a wide variety of shapes and sizes as pots, vases, dishes, and containers. When used outside in a garden or courtyard the materials are applied directly to the surface using an epoxy resin glue for perfect weatherproofing.

▶ Flowerpot (c).
The pot is made of simple white ceramic tiles and rich copper-colored glass and mirror to give an elegantly decorated pot which can be filled with flowers all year round. The design uses an ancient shield-like motif called a pelta.

▲ **Bird Bath. Pedestal Base (a) Fixing.**
*A ready-mixed cement adhesive is made up and, using a small palette knife,
is troweled onto the dry base of the stone pedestal, to a thickness of ¼ in/6 mm,
and smoothly finished.*
*(Alternatively you can make a mortar using the finest sieved sand and cement (3:1)
with added black pigment. These are mixed well together in a dry state, before adding
water. A little of this mortar should then be set aside, and water added to it to make a
slurry. The pedestal should then be thoroughly wetted. Using a brush, apply the slurry
mix to a small area of the pedestal, then trowel a little of the mortar on to the same
area to a thickness of ⅛ in/3 mm.)*

▲ **Bird Bath.
Pedestal Base
(b) Fixing.**
*The tesserae are cut
and fixed into the
mortar, knocking each
"home" with the
mosaic nippers for a
secure fixing.*

cement

Sand-and-cement mortar is an ideal setting
bed for external and large-scale mosaics. It
can be worked in most weathers, and it loves
damp and humid atmospheres. Never work
in frost when the moisture in the mixture can
freeze and expand, causing cracking during
the setting time and interference with the
strength of the cement. Ready-made cement
adhesive is used in the projects,
demonstrating its convenience and versatility.
It can be used on its own or combined with
other setting bases. In this way it is excellent
for interior decorative use.

other bases

Other bases suitable for the direct method
of fixing are card, paper and glass. Decide
first on the location of the mosaic, then the
degree of permanence, and use an adhesive
or binder suitable to bind both the material
used and the chosen base.

◀ **Bird Bath. Pedestal Base (c) Fixing.**
*The base is richly decorated using a mixture of recycled
china and vitreous glass. The effect is dependent on a rich
mix of materials, colors, and textures.*

indirect method

Paper or strong hessian cloth can be used for an indirect method of fixing mosaic. Given the many advantages of the direct method, when the cut surface can be seen at all times, this method need only be used if an absolutely smooth surface is required, or when large-scale mosaics are made in the studio for transportation to a permanent site for fixing, or when tesserae of unequal height but having one flat surface are used in the same mosaic.

▶ **Bird Bath. Bowl**
The bird bath is a shallow stone bowl with its accompanying pedestal base. The indirect method is used for the bowl, since it will be constantly underwater and the mosaic needs to be set into cement for a guaranteed watertight fixing. This method will also give a smooth finished surface.
(a) Fixing.
The tesserae are cut and turned upside down onto strong brown paper for fixing. Give each tessera a small dab of water-soluble gum for a temporary hold. The pattern is a simple circular one, with spaces left for the insertion of glass globules at a later stage to simulate large raindrops, adding to the watery image. The mosaic is made slightly larger than the bowl in diameter to allow for the curve.

▶ **Bird Bath. Bowl**
(b) Fixing.
On completion a ready-mixed cement adhesive is thinly troweled over the dry inside of the bowl. The mosaic on its paper backing is lifted up and carefully placed, mosaic side down, to rest on the cement-rendered bowl. Using a soft cloth and a circular action, the mosaic is gently pressed into the concave bowl and left for a few hours.

◀ **Bird Bath. Bowl (c).**
When you are certain that the mosaic has set into the cement, the paper backing is dampened by wiping over with a cloth, until the paper gently peels off. Take care not to dislodge any tesserae (at this stage any displaced pieces can be recemented into position). The mosaic is then left for 24 hours before grouting and cleaning.

◀ **Bird Bath. Bowl (d) .**
The mosaic is made of vitreous glass tesserae and mirror. The edges of the design were given a scalloped finish.

▶ **Courtyard Ensemble; bird bath (complete), flowerpots, and birds.**

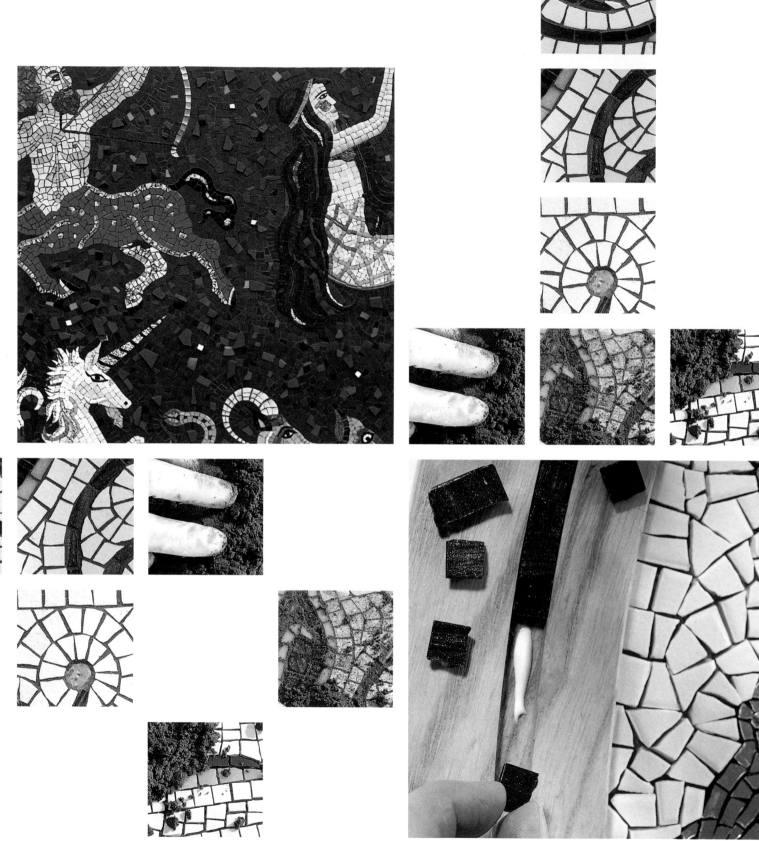

finishing techniques

WHEN THE LAST TESSERAE HAVE BEEN CUT AND PLACED, THE MOSAIC MAY NEED TO BE GROUTED, CLEANED OR SEALED BEFORE BEING PLACED IN A TEMPORARY OR PERMANENT POSITION. THESE PROCEDURES SHOULD NEVER BE RUSHED, BUT EACH CONSIDERED CAREFULLY TO BE SURE OF MAXIMISING THE LASTING EFFECTS OF THE MOSAIC.

grouting

Although traditionally mosaics made of smalti were ungrouted, nowadays most are grouted. This is when the interstices or gaps between the tesserae are filled with a cement mortar – a process that unifies the surface and gives mosaic its characteristic look. Grouting also strengthens the mosaic, giving it an impermeable and moisture-retentive surface.

Grout is a mixture of cement and sand, normally in the ratio of 1:4. The sands may be of any color so long as they are fine-grained sharp sands. They are mixed in a dry state, to which color may be added, if needed. Cement pigment is extremely penetrating and should be added judiciously by the teaspoon rather than bucketful! **Mix the sand,** cement, and color together, taking care to coat every grain of sand with cement; add the water slowly to make a stiff, not a sloppy, mortar, using a trowel to mix. Wearing gloves and/or using a squeegee, press the mortar into the surface of the mosaic, filling all the crevices with the mortar. Take great care over any raised edges. Wipe off any surplus mortar with a damp cloth. Having laid the mosaic on a flat surface to prevent warping, leave to set under a damp cloth or towel for 72 hours. If using a store-bought grout, be sure it has a cement base: this ensures a long-lasting, watertight surface.

cleaning

After allowing the cement to cure slowly in a damp condition for three days (or as instructed on the proprietary brand package), remove the cloths. A surface scum will be seen. Wearing gloves, wash the surface of the mosaic with a diluted solution of hydrochloric acid and water. Add acid to the water in the proportions 1:20. Alternatively, a patio cleaner or a mortar cleaner may be bought which contains hydrochloric acid (HCL). Put some of the cleaner into a nonmetallic container – for example, glass, china, or plastic – and brush carefully over the surface of the mosaic. This should be done outside, and care should be taken to avoid any splashing. A slight fizzing will occur as the acid comes into contact with the alkaline mixture of the cement mortar. Wash the surface and the brushes immediately with copious amounts of water and leave the mosaic flat, to dry off naturally.

sealing

Pebbles and marble and selective mosaic surfaces benefit greatly from an application of a sealant. This has the effect of retaining the true color of the material as if wet, but without necessarily adding a varnish or shine to the surface. Sealants can be bought to retain a matt look or give a "wet" look.

65

framing
Mosaics can be framed in a variety of ways. A frame can help protect and retain the work, and become part of the design. Alternatively, if a mosaic is to be viewed as a "found fragment," an unframed work should be given a resin edge to seal the cut edges and give protection without adding any noticeable frame.

Wooden frames can be made as simple or as elaborate as required. They can be narrow, wide, raised, or flush with the surface, color painted, stained, or varnished. A groove or indentation may be added, into which mosaic material is inserted.

Edgings may be made of metals — aluminum, and steel — or of the mosaic materials themselves. Whole or cut tesserae of glass or ceramic can be stuck and grouted onto the edge. Tile shops also have a variety of edging tiles that can be utilized.

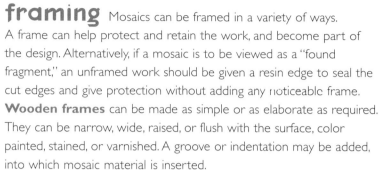

▼ **A wooden frame of white ash with a vitreous mosaic inlay.**
The frame has a groove cut into the surface one-quarter of the width of a tessera. This becomes integral to the overall design.

▲ **Little bird (a).**
A mixture of fine red sand and cement plus terracotta cement pigment was rubbed into the surface to fill up all the gaps between the tesserae. The mosaic frame was grouted at the same time.

▼ **Little bird (b).**
The finished little-bird mosaic is washed clean – the red grouting giving a rich background color.

hanging

If a mosaic is portable, it can be hung by hammering two staples into the backing base, taking care to coordinate their size with the thickness of the wood and the weight of the mosaic. Nylon and steel wire are both suitable materials to support the hung mosaic. Many small mosaics can be hung from picture hooks. Larger works should be hung using mirror plates, or may need to be drilled. The drill holes should be made into the frame or backing, and countersunk before commencing work. When completed the work should be hung in position and the drill holes covered with mosaic for camouflage. If you are creating a sculpture or a three-dimensional piece out of resin or cement that is intended for hanging, insert hooks or hanging loops made out of wire to facilitate this at the time the piece is created.

siting

If working on a floor or ceiling, be aware of the viewing lines, the exits and the entrances, and the angles at which the mosaics are to be viewed — whether they are to be seen at an oblique angle or directly observed, and which of these gives the most engaging impact. If working within an architectural or public setting, be conscious of the need to create an empathy with the building or environment, and emphasize or be sympathetic to the site. Portable mosaics made of mirror or other reflective surfaces respond to oblique placing — adjacent to windows rather than opposite them. Mosaics of both subtle and rich colors should also be sited with careful consideration to enhance and not to diminish or deny their color.

lighting

Mosaics created *in situ* should take full advantage of their unique situation. Historically, mosaicists were well aware of their light source — whether from a window or an artificial source — and tesserae were angled into position toward or against this source for greatest effect.

Artificial light, candlelight, daylight, and intermittent light are all factors that should be considered both before and after creating fixed and portable mosaics, for maximum effect and delight.

▲ **Mythological Creatures (detail), Elaine M. Goodwin and Group 5, St Thomas First School, Exeter, England, 1997.**
Single golden tesserae are angled to catch the light and give maximum brilliance when viewed from the ground, in this large external wall mural.

projects

THE IDEAS FOR THE PROJECTS SPAN 6,000 YEARS OF MOSAIC MAKING, FROM 4,000 BC UP TO THE TWENTIETH CENTURY. THEY ARE IN CHRONOLOGICAL ORDER AND HAVE BEEN INSPIRED BY 16 MOSAICS SEEN BY THE AUTHOR WHEN TRAVELING WORLDWIDE. EACH GIVES AN INSIGHT INTO THE DIFFERENT CULTURE, BELIEF OR PHILOSOPHY THAT WAS UNIQUELY EXPRESSED THROUGH THE MEDIUM OF MOSAIC.

THE MOSAICS USE A WIDE RANGE OF DIFFERENT TECHNIQUES, METHODS, AND MATERIALS IN A STEP-BY-STEP SEQUENCE TO ENCOURAGE EXPLORATION AND EXPERIMENTATION WHEN FOLLOWING THE PROCEDURES. A GRADUAL UNDERSTANDING WILL BE BUILT UP INTO HOW SOME OF THE HIDDEN MYSTERY AND CHARISMA OF MOSAIC WAS ACHIEVED IN THE PAST AND HOW THIS CAN BE ACHIEVED TODAY. IN THIS WAY, MOSAIC MAKING CAN BECOME AN INTEGRAL PART OF CREATIVE EXPRESSION, AND THE SPIRIT OF MOSAIC MAKING CAN CONTINUE TO EVOKE A SENSE OF WONDER AND DELIGHT.

69

Decorated Column

Inspiration DECORATIVE PILLARS. WARKA, IRAQ. FOURTH MILLENNIUM BC.

equipment

- protective wear
- inner cardboard tube from a roll of carpet – diameter approximately 4 in/10 cm
- black enamel paint
- brush
- white household glue
- spatula
- water and cement containers
- ready-mixed cement grout
- patio cleaner
- brush

materials

- ceramic white
- ceramic black
- terracotta vitreous glass
- dark blue vitreous glass

70

Warka (ancient Uruq), to the north of the great river Euphrates in Iraq, is now a silent place. During the fourth millennium BC the city, irrigated by the river, was a garden of paradise. It is here that we find the famous ziggurat, a symbolic pathway between earth and heaven.

The walls of the city were decorated with thousands of colored cones, between 3½–4 in/9–10 cm long. The protruding bases of these cones were colored and arranged in varying geometric patterns, and the colorings may well have been of significance in marking the entrances and exits of the sanctuaries and temples.

method

Paint the tube using a thin layer of black enamel paint. This helps in two ways: it shows up the design clearly as it is created, and also provides a better surface if tesserae have to be removed and replaced while at the same time ensuring a good adhesion to the tube.

1 Cut the white ceramic tesserae into quarter-squares and encircle the base of the tube with three layers of tesserae, as in the ancient original. Use further squares to follow the upward spiraling line of the tube. The spiral is easily identifiable in the makeup of the cardboard tube.

2 Follow the first spiral with a second of two alternate colors. Enclose the second with a third spiral of white tesserae. This strong spiral band will give continuity to the design.

3 Using square units work out on paper three or more designs to fit between the remaining space of the spiral. For example:

1st line: 5 terracotta, 1 white, 1 blue, 1 white, 5 terracotta;
2nd line: 1 white, 3 terracotta, 1 white, 3 blue, 1 white;
3rd line: (4 +) 1 blue, 1 white, 1 terracotta, 1 white, 5 blue.

4 Change the design at approximately every three
complete turns of the spiral. This will give
variety and interest to the pillar as a whole.

5 Continue to make designs that have their own symmetry, as in the original
pillars. Allow each area to dry carefully before each turn of the tube.

6 Continue to mosaic the whole tube. When complete, make up a mortar of
ready-made grout and rub gently into the gaps. Clean with patio cleaner
and water.

The design was made almost completely of cut squares of tesserae. As a first project this will help greatly in practicing the cutting techniques of two frequently used materials: ceramic and manufactured vitreous glass. The designs can be made by beginners of all ages to familiarize themselves with the materials and engage them in a process which has direct links with the earliest uses of the medium. The colors used in this project imitate those of the early columns of Warka, but the pillar may be made of startling color and originality. By making the column, a glimpse can be caught of the possibilities of mosaic making within a three-dimensional and architectural setting. Like the continuing upward spiral, the ways of mosaic are without limit.

Exterior Pebble Step

inspiration PEBBLE MOSAIC. FLOOR, HOUSE OF MOSAICS, ERETRIA, ISLAND OF EVIA, GREECE. FOURTH CENTURY BC

equipment

- protective wear
- paper
- felt-tip pen
- polyethylene sheeting
- fiber netting
- scissors/craft knife
- palette knife
- water and cement containers
- cement adhesive
- cement
- red sand
- cloths
- trowel
- masonry brush
- masonry cleaner
- brush

materials

- white pebbles
- small rose-colored pebbles
- larger rose-colored pebbles
- assorted small black pebbles

The House of Mosaics was built in the late fourth century BC, a Hellenistic Eretrian house that was once home to a ruler. This mosaic is one of two pebble panels which decorated the floor of the *andron*, a room in which symposia and banquets were held. The design has volutes and borders with bands of ivy leaves. The central rosette has a rose-colored center encircled with pairs of coils. A delicate simplicity underlies the design, giving an immediate appeal to the viewer.

Many pebble mosaics are created *in situ* or use a reverse or double-reverse method. However, small-sized pebble mosaics can be made using this direct method. The design should be no larger than 4–5 sq. ft/0.5 sq. meters, since pebbles are fixed to a fiber net and must remain manageable. For the project a semicircular stepped area of 39 in/1 m diameter was used.

method

1 Draw the design on a paper template to fit a predetermined space. A simple design of curved lines was chosen to emulate the ancient Greek vegetal motif. Strengthen the design with a thick felt-tip pen.

2 Put a layer of plastic sheeting and a layer of netting over the drawing. The design should remain very visible. Make up a little of the cement adhesive by adding water and apply to the back of each pebble before affixing to the net.

3 Surround the mosaic with a frame of larger rose-colored pebbles. Use smaller pebbles to create and define the volutes.

4 Use slightly elongated pebbles for the linear drawing.

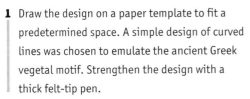
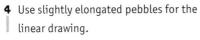

5 Use tiny dark rose-colored pebbles for the central bud and some small elongated black pebbles to give a more delicate and tightly tessellated image.

6 For the white background use white pebbles to follow the outlines wherever possible before completely filling in. When completed, cut the mosaic close to its outer border.

7 The prepared semicircular step should have an indentation of ¾ in/2 cm. Make a quantity of cement adhesive and smoothly trowel over the area to a thickness of ¼ in/6 mm. Drop the mosaic gently into position. Lightly tamp the surface into the mortar using a piece of wood and a hammer. Take care with the smaller pebbles not to let the mortar rise more than halfway up each pebble. Leave the mosaic overnight.

8 Make a grout of three parts fine red sand and one part of cement. Add water slowly to make a thickish mortar. Rub the mixture into the surface, grouting the whole design and the edges. Rub clean using cloths and a masonry brush, then leave to cure under polyethylene sheeting or wet cloths for two to three days before final cleaning and washing with masonry cleaner and water.

The steps are often cluttered with pots of plants and trailing vegetation. They lead down to an area of garden used for outside entertaining, both during the day and in the evening when the white pebbles lightly gleam in the moonlight. Talk often drifts long into the night, recalling the symposia rooms of the original mosaic in Eretria, Greece, where, no doubt, similar conversations were heard and many of the same questions were asked and again left unanswered.

Floor Panel

Inspiration IVY LEAVES. FLOOR PANEL FROM CARTHAGE, TUNISIA, SECOND CENTURY AD, AFTER A COPY OF THE WORK OF SOSOS OF PERGAMUM. NOW IN THE BRITISH MUSEUM, LONDON, ENGLAND.

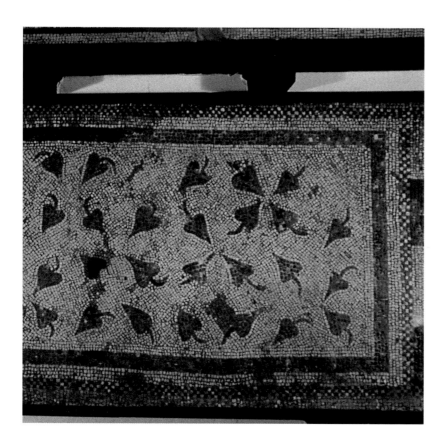

equipment

- protective wear
- paper
- felt-tip pen
- polyethylene sheeting
- fiber netting
- mosaic nippers
- white household glue
- spatula
- tweezers/dental probes
- craft knife
- white tiles 6 in/15 cm
- cement adhesive
- ready-mixed cement grout
- notched trowel
- cloths
- patio cleaner
- brush
- piece of wood approx. 2ft 2 x 5 in/65 x 13 cm for tamping
- hammer

materials

- black ceramic mosaic tiles
- white ceramic mosaic tiles
- plain silver smalti
- rippled silver smalti

One of the most famous of Greek mosaicists in the second century BC was Sosos of Pergamum (Bergama, in present-day Turkey). Renowned examples of his work include "Doves Drinking at a Bowl," and the "Unswept Floor" (*asaroton*) where detritus from a banqueting table is depicted scattered on the floor. Images include fish bones, lobster claws, nut shells, and even a mouse. Many copies of the Sosos originals were made and examples can be seen in Emperor Hadrian's villa at Tivoli and in the Vatican museum, in Rome.

In this mosaic, a copy made in Roman times, black ivy leaves (an image sometimes attributed to the fan of Venus) are randomly strewn over a white ground. They are surrounded by a black band of tesserae and a simple black-and-white checkered border. A wonderful rhythm of shape and direction is created by the stems of the leaves, giving a slightly humorous lilt and life to the whole area.

1 The drawing was done to size to fit a central space 4 x 2ft/122 x 61 cm in a kitchen floor of plain white tiles. Eight leaves were drawn in two groups of four, with a drawing of a running lizard in each. The border was marked by three grid lines which helped when constructing the geometric framing tesserae. The drawing was strengthened by felt-tip pen lines. This was then covered by a polyethylene sheet and then the fiber net. The drawing should remain clearly visible through these layers.

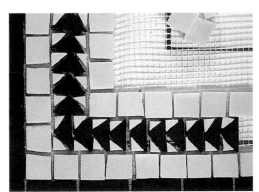

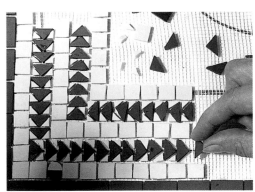

2 Fix whole black mosaic tiles to the surface netting to stabilize the mosaic, and follow by an inner line of white quarter-tesserae. Cut large triangles diagonally from quarters of black mosaic and infill the spaces left with white triangles of half this size. Triangles need perseverance in cutting!

3 Build up the border with two inserts of triangles running in opposite directions – this will accentuate the running theme of the two chasing lizards. Add extra grid lines if necessary to help when constructing the border.

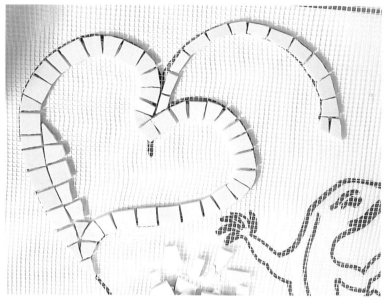

4 Choose to work on the leaves or the lizards next.
Leaves: outline the shape with a single line of white quarters and fill in with *Opus* **Palladianum** – a random tessellation.

5 Cut one black tessera into quarters. Outline the leaf with one line of black tesserae. Take extra care at the tip of the leaf to give good definition.

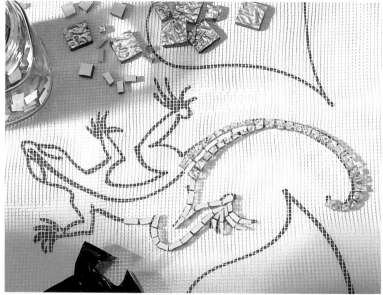

6 Outline all the leaves similarly to give a strong binding form.

7 Lizards: use small squares of rippled silver for the tail and plain for the body.

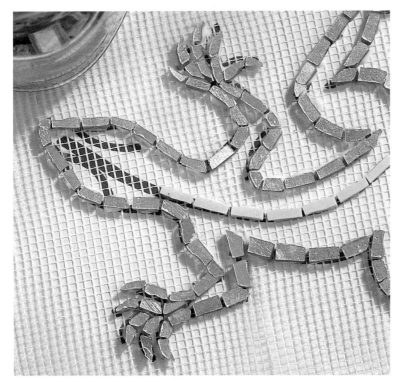

8 Take care in cutting the feet and head shape to give a good silhouette when viewed against the black background. Shape the tesserae to give a good tessellation. It is important when working on small scale images to give good delineation, especially with a limited palette of color.

9 As with the leaves, run a line of tesserae around the lizard's body before filling in the remaining spaces with fairly uniform squares wherever possible, always following a form. When complete, leave the mosaic to dry for at least 24 hours before cutting the net away from the edge of the mosaic as close as possible to the black framing tiles. The mosaic is now ready for fixing.

10 Prepare the cement bed by mixing a quantity of cement adhesive and trowel it level and smooth to ⅛ in/3 mm in depth. Carefully use the notched trowel over the surface to ensure a good gripping adhesion for the mosaic. With help, carefully lower the mosaic on net into its bed. Using the rectangle of wood, slightly wider than the mosaic, gently tamp the mosaic level all over, taking great care over the slightly raised area of the lizards. Leave to set overnight before grouting the work with a ready-mixed cement grout, and clean with the patio cleaner and water as instructed.

The chasing lizards scampering over
the leaves of this mosaic emblema
recall the image of the mouse in the
famous "Unswept Floor" mosaic of
the ancient mosaicist Sosos. They
add incident to an already pleasing
design. The silver set against the
black matt tesserae adds sparkle
and light, enhancing the image of
the chase.

◀ This is part of an
alternative design using
black ivy leaves in a white
ground. The floor is made
to recall the Greco-
Roman era of simple
black-on-white mosaics.
The single golden lizard
emerging into the mosaic
heralds the glowing
Byzantine era to come.
Two great periods of
mosaic are combined in
a single image.

Circular Mirror

inspiration SHELL MOTIF, FLOOR, VERULAMIUM (ST ALBANS), ENGLAND, SECOND CENTURY AD.

equipment

- protective wear
- paper
- ½ in/12 mm plywood, cut to a 30 in/76 cm diameter circle
- compasses
- pencil
- felt-tip pen
- protractor
- ruler
- mosaic nippers
- white household glue
- spatula
- glass cutter
- circular mirror 17 in/43 cm diameter
- ready-mixed cement grout
- patio cleaner
- brush
- water/cement containers
- staples
- two S-hooks
- length of chain
- hammer
- picture hook

The mosaic was originally a floor in the apse of a building made during the first half of the second century. The controlled and skillful use of three colors of Purbeck marble in the fluting of the fan-shaped shell is striking. The marine imagery is carried further by the simplified centrally placed waterfall motif, and the semicircular frame in which the wave crest pattern is used.

The limited palette and the eradication of any extraneous detail make the image at once imposing and unforgettable.

materials

- three shades of white vitreous glass
- mirror tiles
- black vitreous glass

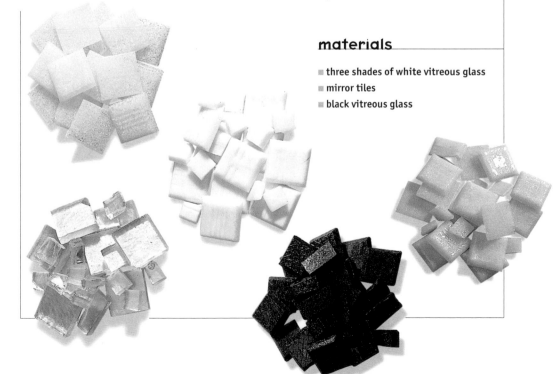

method

1 The drawing was worked out on paper to encompass 16 scalloped edges, thereby giving 16 areas of fluting, each area being at an angle of 22.5°.

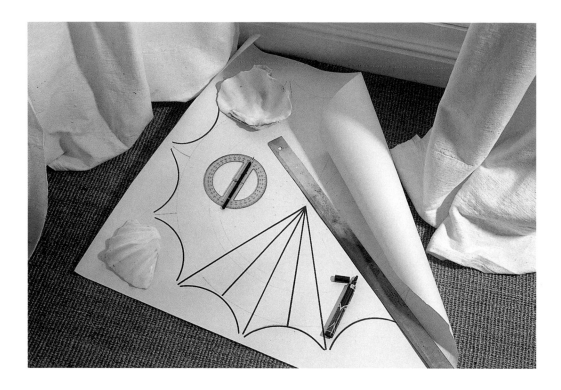

2 Rework the drawing on to the circular wooden base. Use a felt-tip pen to mark the subdivisions. Glue the circular mirror centrally to the wood using the white household glue. Surround with whole mirror tiles. Use the glass cutter or mosaic nippers carefully to make a quantity of irregularly shaped tesserae of mirror and fit them to fill the shape between the scalloped edge and the outer rim.

PROJECTS

3 Outline the dividing lines and scalloped inner edge with the black glass tesserae.

4 Subdivide the segmented sections into three, and use the strongest color in a band three tesserae wide at one side, and the palest color in a band three tesserae wide at the other side.

85

5 Fill in the remaining triangular section with the third shade of the same color. Grout the mosaic with the ready-mixed cement adhesive. Allow to dry. Clean with patio cleaner and water. When completely dry, polish the central mirror.

6 On the base of the mirror tap two staples into the wood, taking care that the length of the staples corresponds with the thickness of the wood base. Use the S-hooks to join the staples to the chain, and hang from a hook positioned on a picture rail.

The mirror, which incorporated at its center a 1930s circular mirror, is hung from a 1930s picture hook in the style of the period. The imagery seemed to evoke the style of that time with its radiating fluted image. The limited color palette emulated that of the Roman period, relying heavily on the gentle optical effect created by the juxtaposition of a muted triple-color palette.

Table Top

inspiration BASKET OF GRAPES. FLOOR DETAIL, EL DJEM MUSEUM, TUNISIA, THIRD CENTURY AD.

equipment

- protective wear
- ½ in/12 mm plywood, cut to a circle of 24 in/61 cm diameter
- felt-tip pen
- compasses
- pencil
- mosaic nippers
- white household glue
- spatula
- tweezers/dental probes
- glass cutter
- ready-mixed cement grout
- water/cement containers
- patio cleaner
- brush
- circular wooden frame of 3 in/ 7.5 cm width
- single leg pedestal bottom

One detail of a large floor in the House of Africa, ancient Thysdrus, El Djem. The mosaic was part of a pavement of linked imagery of food separated into individual panels by braids of foliage and *guilloche* patterning. It is of a luscious basket of grapes. The mosaic was a dining-room pavement adorned with brightly colored designs of food and drink – a mouth-watering and enticing menu of grapes, cherries, dates, and figs. The designs, though simple, have the immediacy and economy of line associated with Japanese still-life paintings – each grape is caught with the simplest of line and coloration.

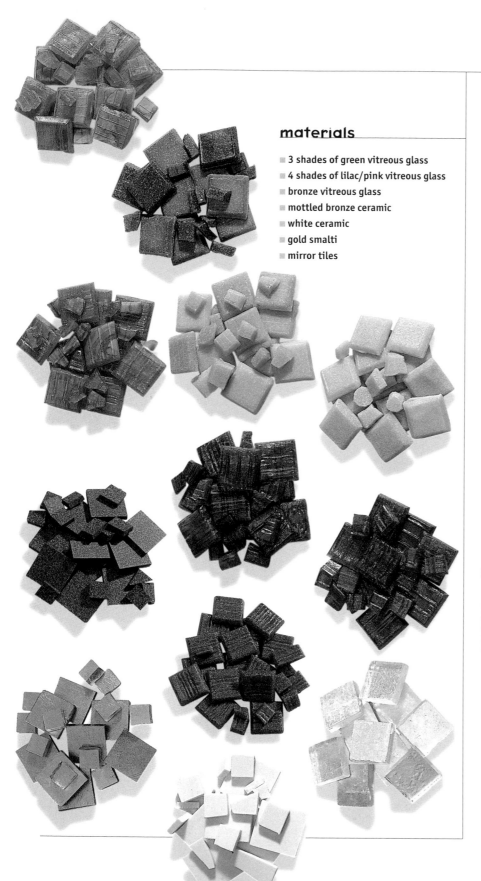

materials

- 3 shades of green vitreous glass
- 4 shades of lilac/pink vitreous glass
- bronze vitreous glass
- mottled bronze ceramic
- white ceramic
- gold smalti
- mirror tiles

method

1 A circle was drawn 3¼ in/8 cm from the outer rim of the plywood. The image was drawn directly onto the remaining central area – two bunches of grapes, two leaves, two tendrils, and one long-stemmed glass. The outer edge represents a basket enclosing the image.

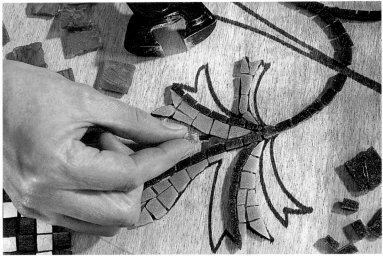

2 Detail of the basket weave. Use gold and bronze squares in a square-and-cross design.

3 Cut the darkest green tesserae into eight pieces to form a drawing or running line for forming the stem and the veining of the leaves. Use a lighter green to form one part of the leaf.

4 Use an iridescent vitreous green to complete the leaf. The dark running line can also be used for the tendrils.

5 The grapes use the lightest lilac for the highlights and remaining shades of pink and lilac for the round grape shapes.

6 Encircle the bunches of grapes with one line of carefully cut tesserae, accentuating the nature of their curved form.

7 Complete the basket weave design by introducing mottled ceramic tesserae. Lay an inner circle of white tesserae to contain the woven geometric border.

8 Cut the mirror tiles with care to form the drinking glass. Introduce a rim of gold. Continue to fill in the background with white tesserae. When completed, grout using the ready-mixed cement grout. Clean with patio cleaner and wash.

The table top explores a design whose surface mosaic is resplendent with bounty, both in the use of materials and in the depiction of imagery. It brings immediately to mind the sumptuous *xenia* mosaics seen on the many floors throughout the Roman empire. Yet the colors are few. Each tessera is used for maximum effect, whether matt or brightly reflective, richly colored or palely glowing, or placed to follow a curve or to become part of a geometric shape. The table invites the onlooker to pick up the glass and drink.

Wall Panel

inspiration BIRDS AT A BOWL AND FOUNTAIN, INNER WALLS, MAUSOLEUM OF GALLA PLACIDIA, RAVENNA, ITALY, FIFTH CENTURY AD.

equipment

- protective wear
- mosaic nippers
- glass cutter
- 12 mm plywood – 25 x 28 in/ 64 x 70 cm
- mosaic tesserae
- white household glue
- tweezers
- felt-tip pen
- pencil
- cement grout
- cutting knife
- cloths
- bowl
- rubber gloves
- water
- masonry cleaner
- spatula

materials

- seven shades of blue vitreous glass
- white/copper vitreous glass
- copper vitreous glass
- mixed white vitreous glass
- white smalti
- white gold
- mirror tiles
- black ceramic tesserae

Pairs of facing birds occur on each side of the drum of the small cupola in the central crossing of the little mausoleum. Two pairs of birds drink from a bowl and two opposite pairs stand by the sides of a small fountain bowl. The image is a classic.

In Roman times the image was made as real as possible, and great attention was given to the sheen of the plumage and the curved golden rim of the bowl. Here, however, the reality of the image is denied. The birds have become symbols, doves of peace. They drink or stand beside the water of life – Christ. The birds are shown in profile with a simplicity of style and color – white, gray, blue, red, and ocher. They are representative of the spirit in all who look at them.

92

method

1 The birds are almost lifesize, and this determines the size of the wood base. The design incorporates both the fountain and the drinking doves to make a composite image, and to accentuate the element of water as an exciting feature of the panel. The drawing should be strong and simple. To acknowledge the unlifelike quality of the image, the drinking bowl was given a rounded base. Outline the whole with a felt-tip pen – this helps to strengthen the design and give an indication of the thickness of the tesserae.

2 You may wish to sketch out and color in a plan for the mosaic. Working with mosaic is an organic process, so you will not need to mark out every piece *per se*, but rather provide yourself with a guide to the outlines, shapes, and colors.

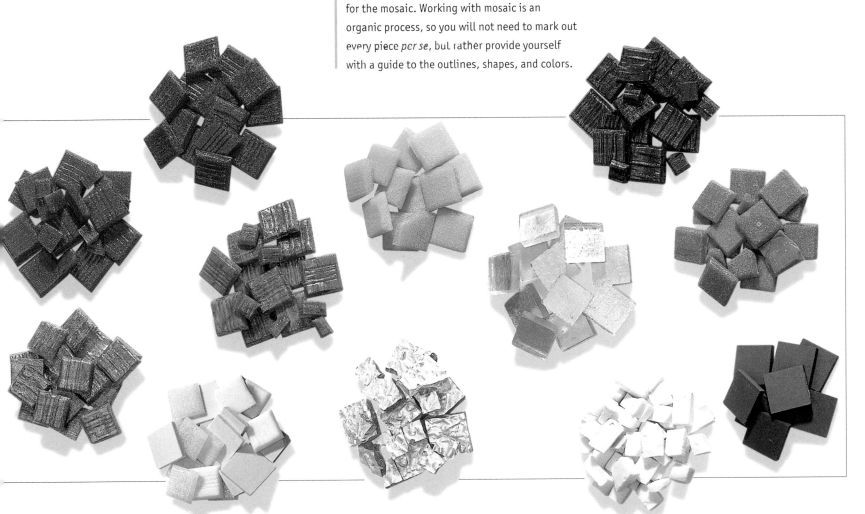

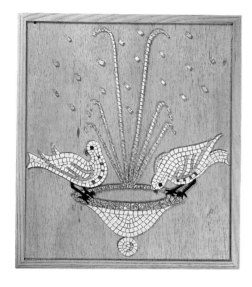

3 Defining the image. Ceramic white tesserae are used to outline the bowl and the birds. Follow the main contours. Use contrasting glass to define the wing shape and eyes. Rippled white gold outlines the rim of the bowl and further rippled gold picks out the curve of the chest, acknowledging the original in Ravenna. Cut the mirror in strips to mark out the upward thrust of the water fountain, and place random pieces of mirror to create droplets.

4 Building up the background. Mark the areas of lighter or darker color, and those of lesser or more textural interest. An area of copper glass forms a divider between ground and background. The lower ground is dark blue with some raised and inverted gold in the corners. This imparts a textural interest to the mosaic surface. The upper background is formalized by an area of white spray, a mixture of ceramic and glass in shades of white. Below this, a graded area of lighter blues deepens to strong blue in the center of the mosaic.

5 Grout with a cement-based grout. In general, richly colored mosaics benefit from a neutral gray grout. Never rush grouting – it is an integral part of mosaic making. Where areas of varying height and material are used grouting takes time and patience. Clean carefully, checking that cement grout is not left in "sunken" areas.

6 Site the mosaic judiciously. Remember in Galla Placidia the Byzantine mosaic artists were working *in situ*, and were aware of the direction of the light from the windows and doors. In artificial light, make full play of the mirror and gold accents in the mosaic to achieve the maximum effect on the lively surface. If placing in natural light, the mosaic should enrich an area and add an extension of coolness and lightness, much in the same way as a real fountain.

7 In creating the birds for the wall behind the garden bird bath, the same materials and method of adaptation were used, but the backing was changed from wood to fiber netting to produce a shallow mosaic. After making the image on the net, the bird shape was cut out using a sharp cutting knife, and grouted on a sheet of plastic. Take care to grout tight into the edges. After curing, clean with masonry cleaner and water. Fix to the wall using a two-part epoxy resin.

The image remains a classic with an appeal which is eternal. The varied background of blues and turquoise with iridescent copper tones provides an intense and rich color backdrop against which the bird images are picked out in bold white "silhouetted" shapes.

▲ In this panel the colors are limited to blacks, whites, and copper tones. The imagery reflects this harmony of color to give emphasis to the silvery and watery highlights of the composition.

Celestial Ceiling

Inspiration STARRY SKY. VAULTED CEILING, MAUSOLEUM OF GALLA PLACIDIA, RAVENNA, ITALY, FIFTH CENTURY AD.

equipment

- protective wear
- ½ in/12 mm marine plywood
- drill
- countersink
- screws
- wall plugs
- white household glue
- spatulas
- palette knives
- mosaic nippers
- glass cutters
- compasses
- pencils
- cement adhesive
- water/cement containers
- trowels
- cloths
- squeegee
- cement grout
- black cement pigment
- masonry brush
- silver/aluminum leaf

materials

- glazed white tiles
- assorted white tesserae
- white patterned china
- glazed black tiles
- assorted black tesserae
- variegated tiles
- thin/thick mirror and mirror tiles
- glass globules

The ceiling is part of a total mosaic scheme in the compact interior of the mausoleum of Galla Placidia. Inside, the ambience is glowing and mesmeric as myriad golden and colored tesserae glimmer in the mellow amber light given by the alabaster windows.

The barrel vault at the entrance is depicted as a celestial sky with hosts of spangled stars in white, gold, red, and light and dark blue on an indigo night background. The mosaic covering is textural, dazzlingly beautiful, and wondrous.

method

The design emulated the starry aspect of the vault of Galla Placidia in Ravenna, using a galaxy of large radiating stars, small six-pointed stars, large rosettes, and tiny mirror domes.

1 Wood was cut to fit a ceiling 11 x 6 ft/3.56 x 1.83 m. It was divided up into 11 equal panels for easier and manageable working. Before commencing work, the wooden panels were fixed in place to the ceiling, and holes drilled and countersunk. The panels were then taken down and the underside numbered according to a continuous plan, 1 to 11, for easy reassembling.

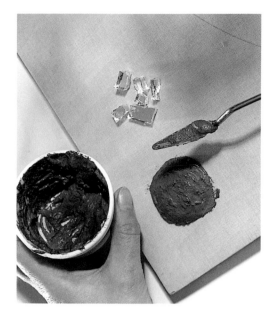

2 For the mirror domes, make up a quantity of cement adhesive to form a thickish paste. Using a pointed palette knife spread a little directly onto the marine plywood, forming a small cement dome.

3 Using the nippers with great care to avoid any splintering, cut the thin mirror into small tesserae and fix to the cement mound.

4 Surround the mirrored mound with black glazed ceramic tesserae in *Opus Palladianum* – irregular-shaped pieces. This material is used solely for the background to create a uniform color on which the stars may shine to greatest advantage.

5 For the rosettes/radiating stars, use an assortment of china, glass tesserae, tile, and mirror. Compass-drawn circles will help mark the layers for fixing the encircling tesserae. Our limitation was one of color – there wasn't any! Just black, white, and silvered mirror. Make the rosettes somewhat smaller than the radiating stars.

6 For the small pointed stars, use simple white tiles for the six-pointed fingers. Keep clear of the countersunk drill holes. Tesserae will be inserted after the ceiling has been fixed in permanent position, to camouflage the fixing points. A glass globule was inserted at the center of each star.

7 Some glass globules are transparent. Rather than allow the wooden base to show through, the glass can be backed with silver leaf. Spread a little white household glue uniformly over the flat back of the glass globule and place on a square of aluminum/silver leaf. Leave for approximately two hours before gently lifting off. The silver leaf has made a perfect metal backing for the glass globule, which can be placed at the center of the small star. When completed, grout – adding black pigment to the grout – and clean and polish with a dry masonry brush before permanent fixing.

The ceiling emits a radiance and sparkle not unlike that experienced in Galla Placidia mausoleum. The materials, however, are not the luscious gold and rich smalti of Byzantium but simple tiles, china, and mirror, much of which was recycled and secondhand.

The china, with its curved surfaces and patterned designs provides a surface rich with reflective power and interest. The little mirror domes catch the movement of those present below – their colored clothing reflected as pinpoints of momentary color. The highly glossy black tiles lend a mystery and depth to the ceiling and as in Byzantine Ravenna a sense of delight and wonder is evoked, which for a fleeting second forms a direct link with the past.

Concept and design Elaine M Goodwin; executed by EMG with Eve Jennings, Glen Morgan, and Rhonwen Vickers.

Bathroom Floor

Inspiration SANDAL MOSAIC.
DETAIL FROM FLOOR OF THE HALL
OF THE SEASONS, MADABA
ARCHAEOLOGICAL MUSEUM,
JORDAN, SIXTH CENTURY AD.

equipment

- protective wear
- strong brown paper
- water-based gum
- brush
- felt-tip pen
- large tile
- quick-setting cement (two hours)
- trowel
- cement/water containers
- hammer
- patio cleaner
- brush
- cloths
- cement grout
- mosaic nippers
- narrow piece of wood longer than the diameter of the mosaic

materials

- white ceramic tesserae
- mirror (copper pink tint)
- black vitreous glass
- black copper vitreous glass
- copper vitreous glass
- white copper vitreous glass
- large white copper vitreous glass

In the garden of the museum at Madaba is a delightfully rendered mosaic representing the four seasons. The colors are bright and bold, and the personifications are naïve and imaginatively interpreted in the corners of a decorative frieze. This is made up of acanthus scrolls encompassing imagery of birds, fish, and goblets.

A white ground of equally large cubed tesserae surrounds the frieze, on which a medallion of a pair of slippers entreats the viewer to take off his or her footwear before walking on the mosaic carpet. It is a request exquisitely proclaimed.

The image is frequently used in Jordanian mosaics and can be seen in a slightly different format in the upper left-hand corner of the Hippolytus Hall mosaic (see page 18).

method

The indirect method was used to ensure an even surface for the bathroom floor when walked upon with bare feet. The floor was tiled, leaving a central circle of 27 in/69 cm diameter. The inner edge was lined with large white copper vitreous mosaic to link both floor and mosaic.

1 Draw a circle of 24 in/61 cm diameter onto brown paper and make up a border of uncut tesserae interspersed with pieces of mirror. Stick these face down onto the paper with a little gum on each. Each section after gluing will benefit from being weighted down by a flat tile or piece of wood to avoid wrinkling the brown paper and help ensure that the surface remains as flat as possible. Cut triangles to fill in at the edges. This will frame and secure the mosaic while you are working. Draw a simple pair of sandals and outline in felt-tip pen.

2 Begin to outline the sandal with a coppery glass mosaic. Keep the outline as true as possible.

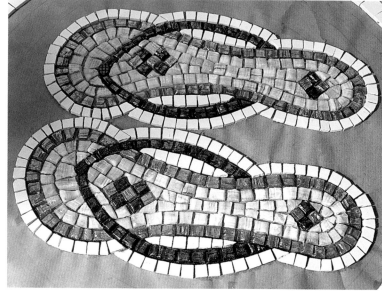

3 Fill in the sandal with a simple pattern design, echoing the diamond shapes in the border.

4 When the sandals are complete, run one line of background white tesserae around both. With small tesserae begin to fill in the background starting with the outer circle.

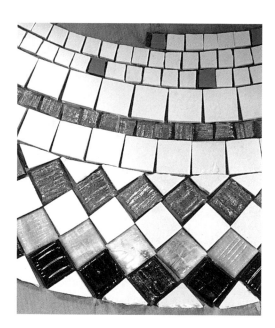

5 At intervals insert mirror tesserae face down. Continue until everything is filled.

6 Prepare the cement bed to take the mosaic. Trowel smooth a setting bed half the depth of the bathroom tiles. With great care, and someone's help, lift the mosaic on its paper backing and position the mosaic face side down on the cement bed. Align carefully, as adjusting impairs the hold and may displace the tesserae. With the piece of wood gently tamp the mosaic into position. It should be flush with the surrounding tiles. Allow to set. Very carefully dampen the paper backing of the mosaic with a wet cloth. After a few moments the paper can be peeled away. Delay this action if the tesserae are not completely held in their setting bed. Should any piece dislodge, gently fix it back into position using cement adhesive. Leave overnight. Grout and clean.

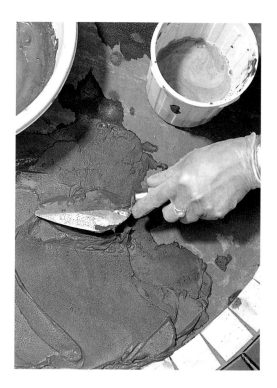

The bathroom was tiled with satin-glazed 2 in/5 cm black tiles, leaving a central circular area for the mosaic emblema or insert. The mosaic became the central feature of the bathroom. The mirror tesserae sparkle and resemble splashes of water as if dripped from a wet body after bathing. The iridescence of the copper tones in the glass tesserae glistens too as if wet, and brings life and fun into the washing routine.

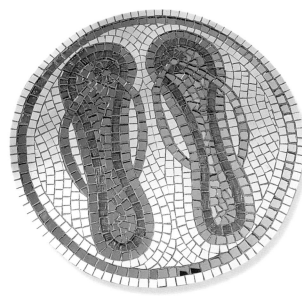

◄ Mirror tesserae define the image of the sandals in this alternative mosaic. Only a hint of color, the turquoise blue, completes the watery theme of the washroom.

Outdoor Niche

Inspiration THE FAÇADE: MIHRAB. CORDOBA MOSQUE, ANDALUCIA, SPAIN, TENTH CENTURY AD.

equipment

- protective wear
- ½ in/12 mm marine plywood cut to the required measurement, 14 x 24 in/35 x 61 cm
- paper
- felt-tip pen
- ruler
- carbon paper
- mosaic nippers
- hammer and hardie
- waterproof white household glue
- brush
- cement adhesive
- water
- palette knives
- wood for inner frame 2 x 1 in/ 5 x 2.5 cm
- drill
- wall plugs
- hammer
- screwdriver
- sealant
- cement sealant
- waterproof glue
- white masonry paint (optional)

materials

- gold smalti/gold chinaware
- 4 shades of blue smalti
- white smalti
- reverse gold- or silver/ aluminum-leaf-backed glass
- white Carrara marble

The mosque at Cordoba is a unique and unforgettable building. Inside is a series of interlocking multilobed and decorated arches which lead to the façade of the *mihrab* (a niche which indicates the direction of Mecca for praying). The glittering façade has a horseshoe-shaped niche opening onto a mysterious and dazzling interior. The exquisite frontage has the effect of arresting the movement of the viewer and preparing and entrancing the state of mind before entering. The interlocking foliate imagery and the broad calligraphic border with golden Kufic lettering on a dark-blue ground are framed within a sculptured marble border. The contrast between the pale marble border and the deep polychromatic and golden mosaic work is stunningly worked to give a controlled and integrated architectural reference to the highly intricate mosaic work.

method

1 Measure the niche. Transfer the measurement to paper. Work out a design to fit the required shape. Keep the design simple but with a certain symmetry. Transfer to the wood using the carbon paper. Firm up the drawing with a felt-tip pen.

2 Seal the cut ends, front and back of the marine plywood. Frame the board with small marble tesserae using a cement adhesive mixed with water to which a little waterproof white household glue has been added. Use the hammer and hardie to cut the marble for delineating the main contours of the design.

3 Use white smalti side end up for outlining the flower forms; this helps to maintain an equal height level with the marble. The smalti adds a certain delicacy to the flower forms.

4 Use the blue smalti and reverse gold to fill in the flower head. The cut edge of the smalti should now be used for these inserts to give maximum reflective power. Continue to use cement adhesive throughout with water and added waterproof white household glue. Be sure to cover the whole area in cement so no wood shows through, because this mosaic will not be grouted.

5 Continue to fill in the mosaic, carefully cutting at any corners.

6 Use the gold for the central features; this will reflect warmly in any external setting. Turn the board around while working. This will greatly assist the placing of the tesserae.

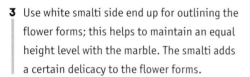

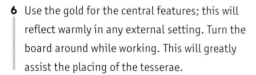

7 Fill in the background with the darkest blue glass. Fit each tessera into the cement individually and progressively for the tightest tessellation.

8 Make up a simple frame to fit the opening of the niche at the required depth, approximately 2 in/5 cm. Fix and seal. The mosaic will be fixed to this using the exterior wood glue: this will ensure a sound and upright fixing for the mosaic. Seal the mosaic surround. If necessary paint any surface surround to correspond with the exterior wall color.

The niche mosaic fits an area in a garden building where once a window existed. In summer the old, east-facing whitewashed walls catch the sun, bathing the site with dazzling noonday light. The mosaic with its Middle Eastern overtones evokes visual memories of eastern journeys and visits to countries that in reality are remote and warmly remembered – precious moments of reflection and recall.

Tree of Knowledge

inspiration THE TREE OF KNOWLEDGE (DETAIL), MONREALE CATHEDRAL, SICILY, ITALY, TWELFTH/ THIRTEENTH CENTURIES AD.

equipment

- protective wear
- ½ in/12 mm marine plywood, 48 x 19 in/122 x 48 cm
- easel
- felt-tip pen
- ruler
- hammer and hardie
- mosaic nippers
- cement adhesive
- palette knives (various)
- trowels (various)
- band saw
- small chisel
- hammer
- cement containers
- waterproof sealant
- brush
- frame (optional)

materials

- red smalti
- pale-aqua-colored smalti
- indigo smalti
- black smalti
- reverse gold smalti/ metal-leaf-backed glass
- assorted gold smalti/ gold-finish ceramic ware
- mother-of-pearl

Stepping into the cathedral of Monreale is like entering a garden of earthly paradise, from the decorated ground up through the slender trunklike pillars to a mosaic canopy of light and color. Each individual tessera of glass or gold is as a bird singing its own tune – the whole interior resonates with light.

After the initial experience of wonder, the narrative within the mosaic work begins to reveal itself. Foremost is the Creation and the Garden of Eden with images of the tree from which came the forbidden fruit, and subsequently the first sin. One image shows the tree laden with bright fruit and foliage with the serpent entwined around the trunk, its head turned toward Eve, the first woman. The figures of Adam and Eve, splendidly naked, one on each side of the tree, are shown at the very minute when Eve gives half of the fruit taken from the tree to Adam, the first man. Their hands are linked through the fruit. It is a moment as powerfully symbolic as that of God and Adam in the painting by Michelangelo on the ceiling of the Sistine Chapel in the Vatican in Rome. It is a moment of innocence before the knowing.

method

The mosaic was done exclusively at an easel in the manner of a Byzantine portative mosaic. For this method, the consistency of the cement adhesive is paramount. It must be firm enough to hold the tesserae, yet not too dry to hinder adhesion. It is messy, too! Persevere – the results are inimitably spontaneous and lively.

1 Cut the wood to size and seal the board and edges with waterproof sealant. Frame the mosaic if required. Draw a tree design around a central axis, directly onto the wood. By working on a vertical surface, great freedom is given in stepping back to view and assess the processes.

2 Cut the smalti in half and begin to draw the outlines, fixing each into a little bed of mixed cement and waterproof adhesive. The mixture should be fairly stiff with no added water.

3 Fill in the leaf areas and the lower trunk of the tree with un-angled gold.

4 Using a band saw, cut squares of mother-of-pearl. To cut the circle, carefully lever a thinnish layer of mother-of-pearl away from its base and nibble around the edges using the mosaic nippers. Press into an area of cement. Surround with red smalti to form the fruits.

5 Cut the smalti on the hammer and hardie for greatest accuracy. It takes time to build up a good rhythm between looking, cutting, and fixing.

6 Continue to work on the red smalti and mother-of-pearl fruits – 13 in all. It may be easier to do the red smalti surround first, before inserting the circular mother-of-pearl disk.

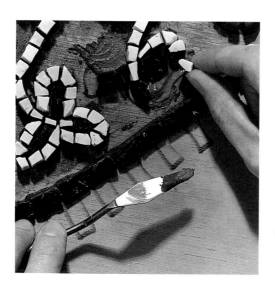

7 Make the smaller trefoiled leaves in the tree canopy by shaping and tapering the tesserae. Place the tesserae on the hardie's chisel edge at the desired angle, but align the hammer with the chisel cutting edge. This may take time and practice.

8 Fill in the background using the indigo smalti interspersed with reverse gold- or metal-leaf-backed turquoise glass.

9 Surround the tree canopy with alternate black and gold tesserae and proceed to fill in the background – all gold. Spread a quantity of cement on to the board using a small trowel (narrow-nosed trowels and palette knives are excellent for awkward angles), and randomly press in the tesserae at varying angles. This will create a surface rich in its play of light.

The completed mosaic shimmers with light. The forbidden fruit gleam with opalescent light, enticing the viewer to inquire or touch. The surface, irregular with smalti of varying heights and angles, and rich with color, inspires a certain reverence for the splendor and seductiveness of its materials. The opulence of the Byzantine period and its desire to employ the mosaic medium for announcing its creed begins to be understood.

italian Mirror

inspiration ALTAR: ORVIETO CATHEDRAL, TUSCANY, ITALY. EARLY FOURTEENTH CENTURY AD.

equipment

- protective wear
- wooden frame
- screws
- drill
- countersink
- wall plugs
- sandpaper
- wood varnish
- brush
- mirror glass, ¼ in/6 mm thick
- white household glue
- spatula

materials

(*alternative materials are given if gold or silver smalti are unobtainable)

- marble tesserae
- gold smalti* (or gold-luster china)
- silver smalti, plain and rippled and reversed* (or mirror tiles)
- alabaster scarabs (or other *objets d'art*)

The façade of the cathedral at Orvieto, a hill town in Tuscany, to the south of Florence, glistens with marble and mosaic gold. The gold has a truly remarkable brilliance. The spiral marble columns and arched doorways are entwined and decorated with colorful mosaic patterning. The stunning combination of white marble features alternating with bands of gold and glass smalti is carried on inside the cathedral, decorating the pulpit and altars. At the side chapel on the north side there is a raised altar or tabernacle with a marble surround that is richly embellished with strips of glistening mosaic. This simple collaboration, combining the purity and strength of the marble with the sumptuous reflective quality of the glass, gives an air of excitement and mystery to the space it surrounds.

(A mosaic segment from the façade of Orvieto cathedral can be seen in the Victoria and Albert Museum in London, and the extraordinary brilliance of the gold smalti examined at first hand.)

method

1 Design and assemble a mirror frame to the shape required to take the mirror glass. It is important to drill and countersink a sufficient number of holes, approximately one drill hole for every 14 in/35 cm, before beginning the mosaic. If possible, affix the frame to the wall by drilling and using the wall plugs, but take down again before starting work. Since a mirror and frame can be very heavy, this will greatly assist the final fixing to the wall. Be sure there is a recessed panel to take the mosaic within a raised border of ¼ in/6 mm depth.

2 Using square and triangular tesserae of differing size, create a design to fit exactly the recessed area.

3 When fixing the tesserae to the wood, keep well clear of the drill holes. After the frame is *in situ*, this area will be covered with the tesserae to create a seamless surface and disguise the fixing points.

4 Instead of continuing the design into the corners, create small areas of interest by including the scarabs (or **objets d'art**, jewels, coins, and so on).

5 On one (or more) of the sides, vary the design. In this case, two larger scarabs were used at the center of a line of smaller scarabs at the bottom of the mirror frame.

▶ An alternative design using turquoise ceramic scarabs from Egypt to create a richly colorful variant.

The proportions and the unashamedly decorative quality of the altar frame – an ornate surround for an altar containing the holy mysteries – led to the concept of using marble and gold for a mirror surround. A mirror is itself a reflective surface with its own mystery and enigma. The materials are similar: gold, marble, and from Egypt, alabaster scarabs, symbols of renewal. The mirror is for a bedroom with an Egyptian element. As at Orvieto cathedral, the shapes of the tesserae are geometric – squares and triangles that are placed lozenge-like to achieve a similar rich, textural effect. The frame in this case is not marble, but of ash, a hard wood. The mirror frame measures 4 ft 8 in x 4 ft 5 in/140 x 135 cm.

Fireplace Panel

Inspiration DOME, THE KARIYE MUSEUM, ISTANBUL, TURKEY, LATE THIRTEENTH CENTURY AD.

equipment

- protective wear
- ½ in/12 mm plywood board measured and cut to fit the fireplace opening, 31 x 34 in/78 x 87 cm.
- strip of edging wood, just under twice the height of the plywood panel
- handsaw
- sandpaper
- ruler
- pencil
- felt-tip pen
- white household glue
- palette knife or narrow spreader
- mosaic nippers
- brushes
- masking tape
- ready-mixed cement adhesive
- ready-mixed cement grout
- cement containers
- gloves
- prodder
- knife
- patio cleaner
- impact adhesive, e.g. epoxy resin for permanent fixing
- tile cement for semi-permanent fixing (this can be removed with a knife)

materials

- gold mosaic smalti or gold-glazed china/rippled gold
- white ceramic mosaic tiles
- black-and-white marble tesserae cubes ½ x ½ in and ¾ x ¾ in (1 x 1 cm, and 2 x 2 cm)

Formerly both a monastery and a mosque, the Kariye Museum (Chora in Ancient Greece) is a small and exquisite jewel among Istanbul's historic buildings. First built in the fifth century, it has undergone many changes and restorations. It is wonderfully decorated with exquisite mosaics and frescoes of the late thirteenth and early fourteenth centuries, created by unknown groups of artists. A rich and magnificent surface is created when the light from the open doors falls upon the irregular golden surfaces of the golden mosaic backgrounds.

This fireplace panel was inspired by the mosaic in the southern dome of the inner narthex. A figure of Christ is depicted in a central roundel with 24 of his ancestors encircling the dome base. The figures are separated by raised ribs of masonry, like spokes of a wheel, covered in rich golden glass. The effect is stupendous – the light catches the raised area and the whole dome appears to revolve and glow with rays of mysterious light. The real sunlight from a side window enhances the effect, playing on the exquisite fluting and giving even more movement.

method

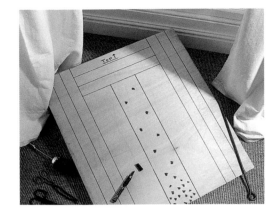

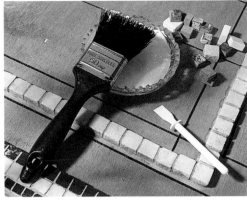

2 Seal the board by brushing the surface with white household glue. Let dry and begin to stick down the marble tesserae with the adhesive, making a wide outer frame and a narrow inner frame.

1 Draw a simple line frame round the board, leaving the bottom area open. Draw two vertical lines dividing the inner central area into three. In the middle panel draw some random marks to simulate and symbolize fire.

3 Grout and clean this area.

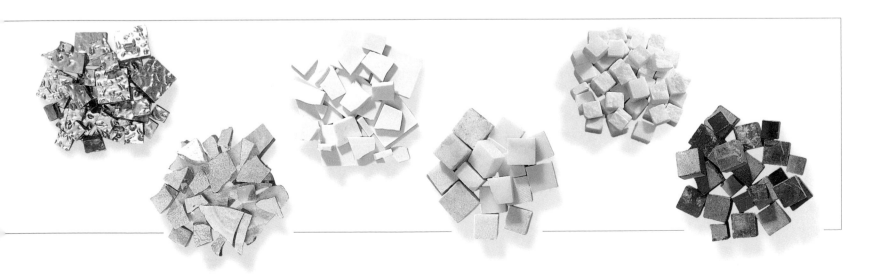

4 Make a thick cement mortar using the cement tile adhesive and adding water carefully. Using a palette knife, spread a layer ⅛ in/3–4 mm thick into the area between the marble framework. Cut the gold material into irregular shapes and press into the mortar, angling the tesserae to catch the light from all directions. This area will not be grouted.

5 Cut the edging wood into two lengths to fit on top of the two remaining vertical lines and glue to the board with the white household glue. Begin to mosaic the outer two panels with a random crazy-paving design (*Opus Palladianum*).

6 Put rippled gold where the firelight marks are drawn. Don't worry if there is a difference in height between the two materials. This also helps to catch the light. Fill in all the background to the panel in a closely tessellated *opus palladianum* continuing to use a matt ceramic mosaic tile.

7 Cover the edging wood with gold tesserae, doing the sides first and then the top. Grout the inner panel carefully, masking the outer area with the tape if necessary. Clean with patio cleaner and plenty of water. Spread the impact adhesive or tile cement onto the edges, reading the instructions carefully, and place in position in the fireplace opening.

The mantelpiece is made of marble with an inner cast-iron fire surround. The mosaic panel was made for when the fire, an open one, was not in use. During the day and in the sunlight, the mosaic screen is like a rich yet restrained abstract panel, its gold gently glowing. At night, in artificial light and with candlelight, the panel scintillates with fiery golds, creating a living centerpiece for the room.

Aztec Pot

Inspiration PECTORAL/CHEST ORNAMENT. AZTEC, CENTRAL MEXICO. FIFTEENTH/SIXTEENTH CENTURY AD. NOW IN THE BRITISH MUSEUM, LONDON, ENGLAND.

equipment

- protective wear
- large terracotta pot 18 in/46 cm in height
- ruler
- felt-tip pen
- paper
- gold-leaf metallic backing
- cardboard
- scissors
- sticky tape
- knife
- epoxy resin adhesive
- sand/glass paper
- cement
- red sand
- red cement pigment
- trowel
- cement/water containers
- cloths
- masonry cleaner
- brush

materials

- mottled red ceramic
- terracotta red ceramic
- white vitreous glass
- copper green vitreous glass
- semiprecious stones: abalone, amber, malachite, gold, mother-of-pearl and agate

The tiny and delicate turquoise tesserae completely cover the front of the looped serpent-breast ornament; the wooden back is flat and undecorated. The rich bluey-green turquoise stone is like a beautifully fitted skin, with directional modulations around the head where red-and-white shell is introduced. Turquoise was much favored in pre-Columbian Middle America and was regarded as a precious and deeply symbolic color representative of a life-giving force through association with water and fertility. The two-headed ornament was worn hung by threads from two holes found in the loops of the serpent's body. The eyes would have been inlaid with precious stones or shiny iron pyrites – an awe-inspiring and sacred object that imparts creative powers to the wearer to rule his people.

method

When using a two-component epoxy-resin adhesive, observe all the manufacturer's safety precautions, wear protective clothing, and work in the open air or a well-ventilated room.

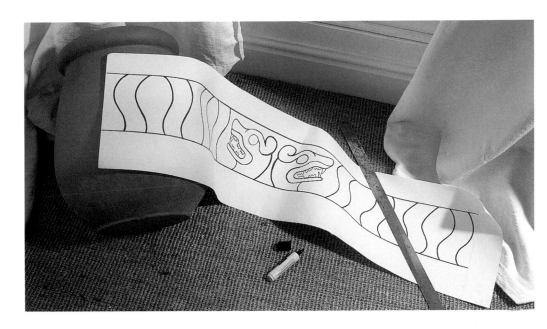

1 Measure the circumference of the pot at its widest part and design a central frieze around this measurement, incorporating a double-headed serpent. Firm up the design with a felt-tip pen.

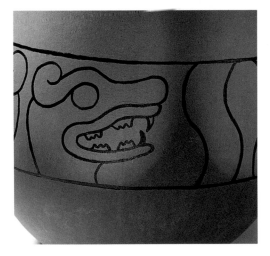

2 Make a cardboard collar for the pot the width and length of the frieze. Slip over the head of the pot to fit the central area, and draw around the upper and lower edges, creating two circular horizontal bands. Transfer the drawing to the pot by cutting out the frieze and affixing it over carbon paper between these two bands, using sticky tape. Trace over the drawing onto the pot. Clarify the drawing by using a felt-tip pen.

3 Use the resin glue to stick ceramic tesserae along the parallel horizontal bands, to give a framing edge for the frieze design. Outline the serpentine curves with white tesserae and begin to fill in the serpent's body.

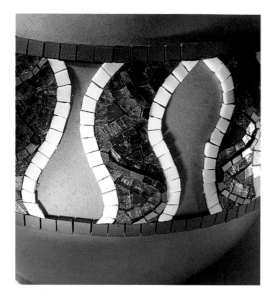

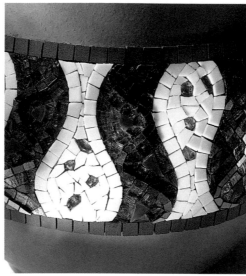

4 Fill in the body adding semiprecious stones.

5 For the white background, insert amber with a gold-leaf backing.

6 Delineate the head using copper-green tesserae.

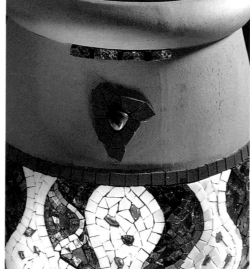

7 Use gold, agate, and other stones for the head, and mother-of-pearl for the teeth. You may find it necessary to use fine sand/glass paper to finely shape the mother-of-pearl for the teeth.

8 Make a band of abalone for the neck of the pot and begin to fill in the background, introducing jade pieces at intervals. Stand the pot on its top when working on the lower areas.

9 A mix of light terracotta tesserae on the darker background will relieve the density of the dark terracotta, yet sustain the rich coloring. When completed, grout using a mixture of red sand, brick-red cement pigment, and cement. Clean.

The pot is exotic and ornate, encrusted with both traditional and mosaic material, and a wealth of semiprecious stones and gold. The tightly contouring skin of terracotta ceramic tesserae which contains the central frieze resembles the curved skin of a serpent. The highly decorative nature of the pot singles it out for admiration among an array of unadorned tubs and terracotta pots on a terrace.

Concept Elaine M. Goodwin; designed and executed by Glen Morgan.

illuminated Letters

inspiration LETTERING DETAIL, THE ALBERT MEMORIAL, LONDON, ENGLAND, 1864–1872.

equipment

- protective wear
- paper
- felt-tipped pen
- carbon paper
- pencil
- strong brown paper
- water-soluble gum
- brush
- wooden board (for working on and tamping)
- sticky tape
- mosaic nippers
- rapid cement adhesive
- trowel
- cement grout
- masonry cleaner
- water/cement containers
- hammer
- masonry paint (optional)

The wondrous extravaganza that is the Albert Memorial was designed by George Gilbert Scott, whose use of gilded metalwork, glass jewels, polished stones, and mosaic work was in turn inspired by reliquaries, altar canopies, and shrines seen while he was traveling through continental Europe.

The mosaics were designed by John Richard Clayton and George Bell and made up by the Venetian firm of Salviati. They cover an immense area of the canopy, the gables, spandrels and inner vaulting, and celebrate the arts with imposing allegorical figures: poetry, painting, architecture, and sculpture. If the figures on their neo-Gothic thrones appear somewhat pedagogic and lifeless to our tastes today, the lettering has a superb animated clarity. The commemorative inscription to the much-lamented Prince Consort runs around the cornice on each of the four faces of the gables:

> QUEEN VICTORIA AND HER PEOPLE
> TO THE MEMORY OF ALBERT PRINCE CONSORT
> AS A TRIBUTE OF THEIR GRATITUDE
> FOR A LIFE DEVOTED TO THE PUBLIC GOOD

– a sincere and fitting tribute to a man who encouraged and supported the arts tirelessly and with imagination. The letters are drawn in dark-blue Venetian glass and in elegant Lombardic capitals on a golden ground. Close inspection reveals an exquisite control in balancing and interpreting the forms of each letter.

materials

- green vitreous glass
- copper-green vitreous glass
- green-glazed tiles
- black vitreous glass
- white ceramic mosaic
- gold/gold-finish china

2 Outline the letters with a running line of black glass and fill in using a combination of green glass and green glazed ceramic. Apply to the brown paper face down, using the water-based gum.

1 Design the logo for a specific external situation. The lozenge-shaped logo measures 24 in x 34 in/61 cm x 86 cm. Strengthen the drawing with a felt-tipped pen on white paper. Move the drawing to brown paper by turning over and tracing through, using carbon paper to transfer the image. In this manner the lettering is conveniently reversed for working on in the indirect method. Firm up the design using a felt-tipped pen. In some cases the design may benefit by being taped down securely to a board for working on.

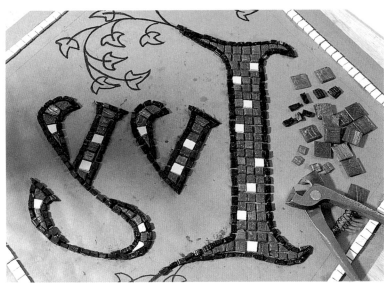

3 In the illuminated letter take special care with the flow of the running line to give a continuous movement. For example, when two lines converge, give dominance to one over the other for the most natural sweep of the line. Frame the design with a single row of white tesserae.

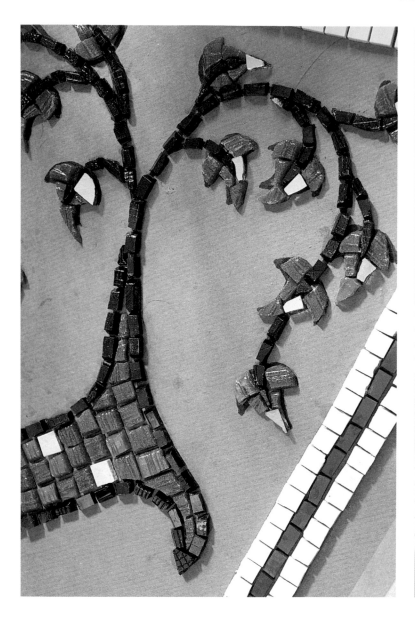

4 Continue to mosaic the stems and trailing ivy forms. In this case the reverse side of the gold was needed and was stuck this side down. Continue to frame the mosaic with one more row of both glass and ceramic tesserae.

5 Outline the letters and image with one line of white background tesserae. Take care around the tiny ivy-leaf contours. When completely filled in and dry, trowel a smooth layer of rapid cement adhesive on to the outside wall. Positioning carefully, transfer the mosaic on its paper backing to the wall, and gently tamp flat with the board. As soon as the quick-drying cement has set, dampen the paper until it peels easily away from the mosaic tesserae. This is a moment of revelation! Clean away any excess cement. Grout and clean. Paint the surrounding wall if necessary.

The diamond shape of the mosaic was determined by two decorative features occurring after the word "Albert" in the mosaic background of the Albert Memorial. The shape resulted in the image gaining greater height and flexibility for the trailing ivy stems of the illuminated letter I.

With a simple color palette of green, white, black, and gold, the sign reads with a delicate elegance and clarity, enhancing the white-painted wall with its clinging ivy and playful shadows.

Concept Elaine M. Goodwin; designed by Eve Jennings and Margot Lublinski, and executed by Eve Jennings.

Art Nouveau Chair

inspiration MOSAIC FRIEZE
"FULFILLMENT", DETAIL,
BY GUSTAV KLIMT. PALAIS STOCLET,
BRUSSELS, BELGIUM, 1906–1911.

equipment

- protective wear
- chair (Inset panels of ¼ in/3 mm depth were designed for the back and seat, and a central groove of the width and depth of one tessera for the back panel. The feet and finial arms were cut back to receive mosaic. Chair height 47 in/120 cm; depth 14 in/36 cm; width 10½ in/ 27 cm.)
- white household glue
- spatula
- mosaic nippers
- sketchbook
- drawing pen
- pencil
- felt-tip pen
- hammer
- furniture glides
- cement grout
- cloths
- containers
- patio cleaner
- brush

materials

- copper-pink vitreous glass
- pink ceramic
- green vitreous glass
- reverse gold
- pink gold
- gold
- white vitreous glass
- white ceramic

The Austrian artist Gustav Klimt made an inspirational visit in 1903 to view the mosaics in Ravenna, Italy, in connection with a commission to create a dining-room frieze. This was for the industrialist Adolphe Stoclet at his Brussels town house, designed for him by the architect Joseph Hoffman.

Klimt applied decorative elements to all he created – paintings, textiles, furniture, textile patterns, dress designs, dinner services, jewelry, and mosaics – evolving a rich pantheon of symbols. Through these he expressed his love of the sensuous and the sexual, which were the mainspring of his existence.

The mural décor is elegant and luxurious with precious metals – above all, gold. The mosaics were carried out under his supervision by the Wiener Werkstätte, an Austrian association of which Klimt was a founder member, and were installed in 1911. The frieze depicts a couple joined in an all-encompassing embrace against a background of golden spirals and tendrils emanating outward horizontally from a tree whose roots are deeply embedded in a ground fertile with symbols and ornamental imagery. The work comprises mosaic gold and glass, painted areas, and unique tiles created by Klimt in exquisite colors and textures.

method

1 Draw a simple sketch for this mosaic design. The concept was based on the human figure.

2 Transfer the design to the chair, carefully drawing the finished result in felt-tip pen. Begin work on the golden spirals, cutting larger tesserae to accentuate any particular volutes. Begin covering the inset area at the feet and finial arms with squares of golden tesserae.

3 Mosaic the inner and outer sides first, before adding the front and back sections. In this way the backing glass of the gold is disguised.

4 Continue to mosaic the front and back. Hammer furniture glides centrally on the base of each leg. (These protect and lift the chair from direct contact with the floor.)

5 Introduce a design of green and pink color for the front spine of the chair and its continuation into the seat area.

6 Elaborate the design in the seat area. This can be of symbolic or personal reference.

7 Introduce the white tesserae for the central background panel. The ceramic material contrasts and heightens the reflective qualities of the metal and glass used.

8 Follow the volutes as they curve in spirals and tendrils.

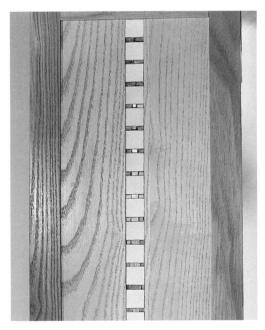

10 Start to fill in the recessed groove at the back of the chair if there is one.

9 Fill in using alternate white glass and ceramic.

11 A ladder-back design of ceramic, gold, and reverse gold was inserted.

The chair pays an open homage to the Art Nouveau period, with its elongated elegance and its applied decorative features. The spiral, a symbol so beloved of Klimt, is used with true symbolic reference alongside further ornate and sensual elements. Sumptuous use was made of gold and glass, to resonate, dazzle, and delight. We are indeed in the realms of art and artifice.

Concept, design and execution by Elaine M. Goodwin; chair made by Vic Mousel.

Wall Sculpture

Inspiration ANTONIO GAUDÍ, LIZARD FOUNTAIN, PARC GÜELL DETAIL, BARCELONA, SPAIN, 1900–1903.

equipment

- protective wear
- lizard sculpture (either make it yourself or buy a ready-made garden center sculpture, about 18 in/46 cm)
- 4B pencil
- cement adhesive
- waterproof white household glue
- trowel
- water/cement containers
- palette knife
- mosaic nippers
- knife
- dental tweezers/probes
- ready-mixed cement grout
- masonry cleaner
- brush
- cloths
- masonry brush
- wire } (optional)
- scrim/glaze }

The genius of the Spanish architect and artist Antonio Gaudí was allowed to flower under the patronage and friendship of that most wealthy Catalan industrialist and nobleman, Don Eusebio Güell i Bacigalupi. Inspired by English garden cities, Güell decided to instigate the creation of a garden suburb, and commissioned Gaudí to join with him in realizing this vision. The plan failed, but the world gained an extraordinary and wondrous public garden.

Spain is famed for its tiles, a legacy enhanced by the Arab conquests from the eighth century. Gaudí used this ceramic material almost exclusively to add color, texture, and vibrancy to his creations, alongside glass and found objects. Much of his work is sculptural, introducing more fully a new area for the mosaicist to explore, with curves, spheres and cylindrical shapes. This extra dimension adds diversity and versatility to the mosaic medium, which could now be placed in space externally and internally. The lizard fountain initiates and welcomes each visitor who enters this park of Art within Nature.

method

materials

- assorted golden- and orange-colored china, tile, luster-ware, gold
- assorted green china
- assorted turquoise earthenware, glass, reverse silver (blue metal-leaf-backed glass)
- assorted red china, tile

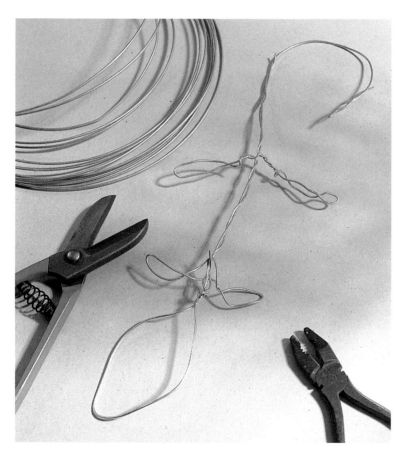

1 Much of the material used for the lizard was recycled or from broken chinaware, plus a miscellany of found materials. Make the lizard sculpture yourself using a wire frame, cement, and scrim/gauze, or buy a similar ready-made sculpture from a garden center.

2 The lizard was coated with a layer of cement adhesive to give a sound, clean, and smooth binding base for the mosaic. Add water to the cement adhesive and brush on.

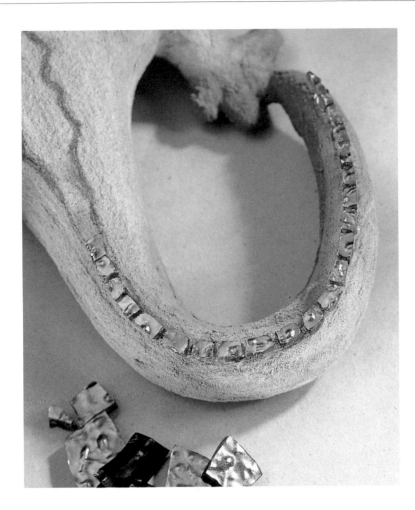

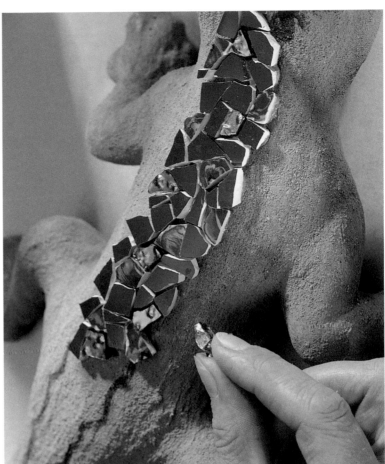

3 Very simple guidelines were drawn on the back of the lizard with soft pencil marks. Cement adhesive mixed with waterproof white household glue was used to fix the central golden spine on to the tail.

4 Cut small tesserae of china and fix to the back area.

5 Vary the china for the head, and delineate the eye area. The eyes were glass eyes from a market in the Middle East – protective talismans against evil.

6 Use assorted materials to give a rich texture and color.

7 Continue to mosaic the tail area. The fluted border of a plate gave added interest.

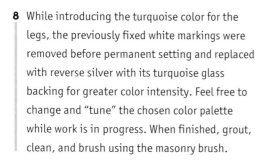

8 While introducing the turquoise color for the legs, the previously fixed white markings were removed before permanent setting and replaced with reverse silver with its turquoise glass backing for greater color intensity. Feel free to change and "tune" the chosen color palette while work is in progress. When finished, grout, clean, and brush using the masonry brush.

The finished lizard basks in the sun on a well-warmed wall – its colors fiery and glowing. The once pale and understated garden creature revels in a shiny new skin. Broken, discarded, and replaced china and tiles celebrate their regeneration in a riot of color combinations. Post-Gaudí, mosaic has a new and endearing evaluation of materials, place, and application.

▲ The lizard reconnoiters among the vegetation of the garden.

author's work
and inspiration

THE FIGURATIVE AND ABSTRACT WORKS SHOWN WERE MADE AFTER FREQUENT VISITS TO OTHER COUNTRIES. SOME OF THE WORK HAS USED ARTIFACTS AS A STARTING POINT, WHILE OTHERS HAVE EVOLVED FROM DIRECT OBSERVATION AND EXPERIENCE OF NATURE, AND TRANSLATED INTO MOSAIC THROUGH STONE AND GLASS.

▼ **Title:** *He*, 1995, 39 x 39 in (100 x 100 cm).
Materials: *Carrara marble, smalti, antique gold, fool's gold.*
Technique: *Direct method into cement on a wood base.*
Inspiration: *Sculpture from the Archeological Museum (Arkeoloji Muzesi) Istanbul, Turkey. A celebration of the parts. The torso makes a compact statement accentuating the anonymity of the figure, while the horizontal bands allude to the infinite. It is a timeless appraisal in glass and stone.*

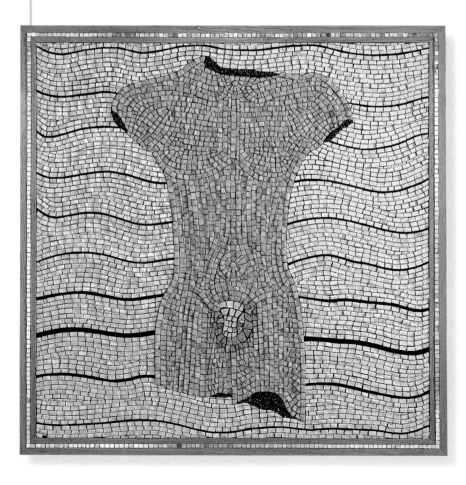

▲ **Title:** *Gates of the Living I*, 1992, 34 x 39 in (85 x 100 cm).
Materials: *Marble, smalti, Venetian white gold, vitreous glass, granite.*
Technique: *Direct method onto wood and grouted.*
Inspiration: *One of a series of three works completed after extensive visits to Egypt exploring the many temples and painted tombs, and appreciating the ancient Egyptians' unquestioning confidence in the afterlife. The work expounds the cyclic movement of energy and life using a tree as a channel.*

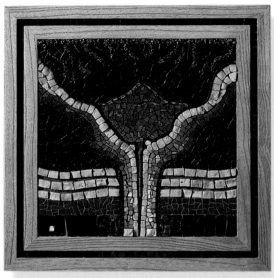

▲ Title: *Preliminario I*, 1997, 16 x 16 in (41 x 41 cm).

▲ Title: *Preliminario II*, 1997, 16 x 16 in (41 x 41 cm).

Materials: *Smalti, Venetian gold, marble, granite, alabaster, vitreous glass, ceramic, fool's gold. Siwan sand is used in the grouting (I).*
Technique: *Direct into cement on wood and partially grouted.*
Inspiration: *Two works resulting from a memorable visit to the oasis at Siwa in Egypt's Western Desert. Here is the most ancient of oracles, consulted by Alexander the Great directly after he had founded the city of Alexandria. They are poems of exploration at moments of exquisite pleasure.*

◀ Title: *Night Blues*, 1995, 20 x 61 in (50 x 156 cm).
Materials: *Smalti, Venetian gold, marble, vitreous glass.*
Technique: *Direct method onto wood and partially grouted.*
Inspiration: *The National Museum of Tokyo, Japan. One of a series of four works in vertical format recalling both the delicate scroll paintings of Japan and the soaring architecture of this highly technological society. The central insert panel, like a circuit, acts as a mandala and lamentation to the Japanese society – hence the Blues.*

▶ Title: *Luccichii di Venezia: Amando*, 1992, 27 x 27 in (68 x 68 cm).
Materials: *Smalti, Venetian gold, vitreous glass, fool's gold, granite.*
Technique: *Direct method onto wood and partially grouted.*
Inspiration: *One of a series of six works inspired by the ephemeral nature of Venice, Italy. Using the vine as a metaphor, the ubiquitous watery nature of the city invited reflection.*

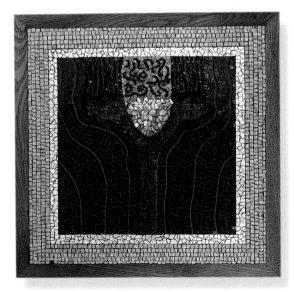

other sites
and sources of inspiration

ancient

THE BRITISH MUSEUM, LONDON, ENGLAND

THE BERLIN STATE MUSEUM, GERMANY

THE NATIONAL MUSEUM, CAIRO, EGYPT

ancient greek

OLYNTHUS, GREECE

AMPURIAS, SPAIN

DELOS, GREECE

roman

THE GRAECO-ROMAN MUSEUM, ALEXANDRIA, EGYPT

ANCIENT CORINTH, SITE AND MUSEUM, GREECE

NATIONAL MUSEUM, NAPLES, ITALY

SANCTUARY OF FORTUNA PRIMIGENIA, PRAENESTE, ITALY

OSTIA, ITALY

PIAZZA ARMERINA, SICILY, ITALY

THE VATICAN MUSEUM, ITALY

THE IMPERIAL/GREAT PALACE, MOSAIC MUSEUM, ISTANBUL, TURKEY

THE WOODCHESTER PAVEMENT, GLOUCESTERSHIRE, ENGLAND

LEEDS CITY MUSEUM, ENGLAND

▲ **Fishbourne Palace, Sussex, England.**
Detail showing the guilloche *or braiding pattern*

SOMERSET COUNTY MUSEUM, TAUNTON, ENGLAND

CONSTANTA, BLACK SEA, ROMANIA

TOSSA DE MAR, SPAIN

ITALICA NEAR SEVILLE, SPAIN

RHEINISCHES LANDESMUSEUM, TRIER, GERMANY

PALACE OF DIOCLETIAN SPALATO,

BAALBEK, LEBANON

VILLA OF CONSTANTINE, ANTIOCH, TURKEY

paleo-christian

NATIONAL MUSEUM OF RAVENNA, ITALY

CATHEDRAL OF AQUILEIA, ITALY

SANTA COSTANZA, ROME, ITALY

MAUSOLEUM OF CENTCELLES, TARRAGONA, SPAIN

NECROPOLIS, ST PETER'S, ROME, ITALY

byzantine

HAGIA SOPHIA, ISTANBUL, TURKEY

HAGIOS GEORGIOS, SALONIKA, GREECE

CHURCH OF HOSIOS DAVID, SALONIKA, GREECE

CATHEDRAL OF CEFALÙ, SICILY, ITALY

CATHEDRAL OF PALERMO, SICILY, ITALY

BAPTISTRY OF SAN GIOVANNI, FLORENCE, ITALY

SAN MINIATO AL MONTE, FLORENCE, ITALY

PISA CATHEDRAL, ITALY

SS. MARIA E DONATO, MURANO, VENICE, ITALY

CATHEDRAL OF TORCELLO, VENICE, ITALY

SAN APOLLINARE IN CLASSE, RAVENNA, ITALY

SAN APOLLINARE NUOVO, RAVENNA, ITALY

SANTA MARIA MAGGIORE, ROME, ITALY

SAN CLEMENTE, ROME, ITALY

SS. COSMA E DAMIANO, ROME, ITALY

ST CATHERINE'S MONASTERY, SINAI, EGYPT

SANTA SOFIA, KIER, RUSSIA

pre-columbian

BRITISH MUSEUM, LONDON, ENGLAND

NATIONAL MUSEUM OF ANTHROPOLOGY, MEXICO CITY, MEXICO

PIGORINI MUSEUM, ROME, ITALY

post-renaissance

THE GILBERT COLLECTION, USA

THE HERMITAGE, ST PETERSBURG, RUSSIA

victorian and later ...

VICTORIA AND ALBERT MUSEUM, LONDON, ENGLAND

THE OPÉRA, PARIS, FRANCE

ST PAUL'S CATHEDRAL. LONDON, ENGLAND

WESTMINSTER CATHEDRAL, LONDON, ENGLAND

art nouveau

CATHEDRAL OF THE SAGRADA FAMILIA (A. GAUDÍ), BARCELONA, SPAIN

CASA BATLLÓ, CASA MILA (A. GAUDÍ), BARCELONA, SPAIN

THE SECESSIONIST BUILDING (J. OLBRICH), VIENNA, AUSTRIA

the naïves

THE JUNK GARDEN OF BODAN LITNANSKI, VIRY NOUREUIL, NORTHERN PARIS

CHILDREN'S SCHOOL FAÇADE, COLUMBIA ROAD, LONDON, ENGLAND

public mosaic

▲ Detail, Tottenham Court Road Underground Station, London, England. Eduardo Paolozzi.
Detail showing areas of smalti against a utilitarian white background. The imagery is of music and rhythm.

SARDINIA; MARIA GRAZIA BRUNETTI

SNAIL FOUNTAIN, S. AGATA FELTRIA, ITALY; MARCO BRAVURA

FUNERAL SCULPTURE OF RUDOLPH NUREYEV, CEMETERY OF S. GENEVIÈVE SOUS BOIS, PARIS (CARRIED OUT BY AKOMENA RAVENNA)

◀ Lantern of the Dome, St Peter's, Rome, detail, late sixteenth/early seventeenth century.
This detail from the Lantern of Michelangelo in the Basilica of St Peter's shows that some mosaic work continued to be created alongside frescoes, painting, and sculpture – work whose effects are unique to mosaic.

suppliers

Many of the materials used in mosaic making can be found at builders' supply stores, hardware specialists, and tile shops. Suppliers and stockists of specialist materials are listed below.

Australia

GLASS CRAFT AUSTRALIA
54-56 LEXTON ROAD
BOX HILL NORTH
VICTORIA 3129
TEL: (61) 3 9897 4188
FAX: (61) 3 9897 4344

ALAN PATRICK PTY LTD
11 AGNES STREET
JOLIMONT
VICTORIA 3002
TEL: (61) 3 9654 8288
FAX: (61) 3 9654 5650

Canada

CERAGRÈS
9975 BLVD ST LAURENT
MONTRÉAL
QUÉBEC. H3L 2N5
TEL: (1) 514 384 2225
FAX: (1) 514 384 4415

OLYMPIA TILE
1000 LAWRENCE AVENUE WEST
P.O. BOX 1215
STATION T
TORONTO
ONTARIO. M6B 4AA
TEL: (1) 416 785 6666
FAX: (1) 416 789 5745

PAINT INSPIRATIONS
2003 WEST 4TH AVENUE
VANCOUVER
B.C. V6J 1N3
TEL: (1) 604 737 8558
FAX: (1) 604 737 8101

France

OPIO COLOUR
4 ROUTE DE CANNES
06650 OPIO
TEL: (33) 04 93 77 23 30
FAX: (33) 04 93 77 40 56

italy

MARIO DONA E FIGLI SNC
VIA MARCHETTI GUISEPPE 6
33097 SPILIMBERGO (PN)
FRIULI
TEL/FAX: (39) 0427 51125

MOSAICI DONÀ MURANO
STEFANO DONÀ
FONDMENTO VENIER. 38/A
30141 MURANO
VENEZIA
TEL: (39) 41 736 596
FAX: (39) 41 739 959

FERRARI & BACCI SNC
VIA AURELIA 14
55045 PIETRASANTA (LU)
TOSCANIA
TEL: (39) 584 790147
FAX: (39) 584 794182

United Kingdom

PAUL FRICKER LTD
WELL PARK
WILLEYS AVENUE
EXETER EX2 8BE
TEL: 1392 278636
FAX: 1392 410508

LANGLEY LONDON LTD
THE TILE CENTRE
161–167 BOROUGH HIGH STREET
LONDON SE1 1HU
TEL: (44) 171 407 4444

TOWER CERAMICS
91 PARKWAY
CAMDEN TOWN
LONDON NW1 9PP
TEL: (44) 171 485 7192

EDGAR UDNY AND CO. LTD
THE MOSAIC CENTRE
314 BALHAM HIGH ROAD
LONDON SW17 7AA
TEL: (44) 181 767 8181
FAX: (44) 181 767 7709

United States

AQUA MIX (FOR SEALANTS)
PO BOX 4127
SANTA FE SPRINGS
CA 90670
TEL: (1) 562 946 6877
FAX: (1) 562 944 8873

MOSAIC MERCANTILE
MODERN OPTIONS INC.
2831 MERCED STREET
SAN LEANDRO
CA 94577
TEL: (1) 410 483 9962

index

143

► *Detail of spiral facade column, Orvieto Cathedral, Orvieto, Tuscany.*